10699123

YOU SAY POTATO

BEN CRYSTAL AND DAVID CRYSTAL

YOU SAY POTATO

A BOOK ABOUT ACCENTS

MACMILLAN

First published 2014 by Macmillan
an imprint of Pan Macmillan, a division of Macmillan Publishers Limited
Pan Macmillan, 20 New Wharf Road, London N1 9RR
Basingstoke and Oxford
Associated companies throughout the world
www.panmacmillan.com

ISBN 978-1-4472-4969-6

3 5 7 9 8 6 4 2

A CIP catalogue record for this book is available from the British Library.

Printed and bound by CPI Group (UK) Ltd, Croydon, CR0 4YY

Visit **www.panmacmillan.com** to read more about all our books
and to buy them. You will also find features, author interviews and
news of any author events, and you can sign up for e-newsletters
so that you're always first to hear about our new releases.

CONTENTS

For Emma P, Jon B, and Cathryn S, without whom . . .
And for Momma C/Hilary

PROLOGUE: AT HOME WITH THE CRYSTALS

BEN I must have been around sixteen years old when I walked into the house I grew up in and unwittingly dropped a linguistic bombshell.

As I strolled into the kitchen, slung my school bag down and began to make a cup of tea, my father immediately stopped what he was doing, looked up, and raised his (not inconsiderable) eyebrows.

I checked about me. There was no original copy of Johnson's *Dictionary* on my person, nor did I have one of the fabulously rare original Shakespeare First Folios in my satchel. I was not wearing my *To split, or not to split, that is the infinitive* . . . T-shirt; I hadn't left the milk out, or the tea-bag in.

Clearly, then, I must have *said* something interesting.

Dad frowned, like a baffled but not unkindly owl, eyebrows still hovering a few inches above his spectacles. He leaned forward excitedly, as an entomologist might if a beetle had suddenly rolled over onto its back and held aloft a tiny sign which read 'tickle my tummy'.

D – What did you say, Ben?

I shifted uncomfortably as I tried to recall what I'd

muttered that had piqued his interest. This, it should be noted, was not a new phenomenon. Over the previous couple of years, I had, it seemed, returned to the house with an assortment of linguistic fascinations, sweetmeats, and chew-toys for my father.

Wicked – meaning 'fantastic' – dominated one family meal. *Dark* – as a negative happening – compassed an entire weekend. An experiment (when I was twelve) over Sunday lunch with a word whose meaning I wasn't entirely sure of ('git') quickly brought me to the realization that, whatever it meant, it was not complimentary.

I thought back to what I'd said when I walked in the door, and ran over it again in my head. I couldn't think what it might be. So I mumbled the whole phrase once more, and, of course, foolishly fell down the rabbit hole.

– I said, I hate my new school schedule. It's all doubles, and *Frau* Schmidt, if that's her *real* name, which I *doubt*—

D – Schedule?

I blinked.

– Yeah. My new schedule.

D – Schedule?

– Yeah. Schedule.

D – Schedule.

– Daaaad. Schedule.

This was like taking some sort of lie-detector test, or being grilled by Scientologists. The repetitiveness was beginning to numb my brain.

D – You mean . . .

And here the shark showed its teeth.

D – Shhhhedule?

– Yeah . . . I said cautiously, aware of the ground starting to slip under my feet. 'S what I said. Schedule, I mumbled.

D – Ah no, ha, you said *skedule*.

– Yeah. Skedule, shedule, Shrewsberry, Shrowsberry, sconn, scown. What's the diff?

D – The diff, my boy, he said, getting up to pour me a rather adult-looking glass of wine, is America.

And then I sat down, and we began talking about why.

DAVID   I have to say it did surprise me when I first heard Ben say 'skedule'. And I was also surprised to realize that *he* didn't realize where his pronunciation had come from. It wasn't like the two pronunciations of *scone* or the two of *Shrewsbury*. They have histories arising out of the way different accents have developed in Britain. No, this was, indeed, one of the first signs that American English pronunciation was beginning to have a long-term impact on British English accents. Because it wasn't just Ben who was saying this. All his friends were too.

And, eventually, the rest of my four children. There was an interesting transitional period, somewhere in the early 1990s, when the two eldest ones (a decade older than Ben) were saying 'shedule', and the two youngest ones were saying 'skedule'. But they all say 'skedule' now.

As do I – when I'm talking to them. And when I'm not, I continue to say 'shedule', on the whole. So I have two pronunciations of this word in my repertoire these days. My personal speech is a sign of transitional times: the Old Pronunciation World meeting the New.

Why the early 1990s? In fact, people had begun to use the American pronunciation of this word earlier, but it was sporadic and idiosyncratic, reflecting individual encounters with American English. Any Brits who had spent some time in the US, and who enjoyed the experience, would probably come back with their accent modified in some way. But Ben had never been to the US, and was illustrating something that was affecting a whole generation. What caused that?

In a word, TV. And especially sitcom TV. Just think of the way in which American sitcoms arrived on British television from the 1950s onwards. The oldest readers of this book will remember *I Love Lucy*, first aired in 1951. Slightly less old readers will have happy memories of *The Munsters*, *The Monkees*, and *The Addams Family*, all from the sixties. Then the sitcom numbers rapidly grew. Among the most popular in the seventies were *The Brady Bunch* and *M*A*S*H*. In the eighties, *The Cosby Show* and *Cheers*. As Ben became a teenager, he watched several of these. It was the TV era. The Internet was still a decade away. And then, at the very end of the eighties, the Really Big One: *The Simpsons*.

But actually, Ben's 'skedule' couldn't have come from *The Simpsons*, as – if the online scripts are to be trusted – none of the characters use that particular word at all in the episodes aired in the first few years of the show. But it does turn up in other series that he was watching at the beginning of the 1990s, such as *Northern Exposure*. The pilot episode in 1990 sees Joel, a New York doctor newly arrived in a town in

Alaska, wanting to leave by bus. Ruth-Ann asks him, 'Would you like a schedule?' And we hear the word again a few seconds later when Joel tries to escape from his waiting patients: 'I have a bus schedule,' he says. *Sked-* both times.

Schedule, of course, is just one of several American pronunciations that have spread around the English-speaking world. Think of *anti-* rhyming with *tie* rather than *tea*, or *ate* rhyming with *late* rather than *let*. Think of the second syllable of *tomato* sounding like *mate* rather than *maht*, or the first syllable of *progress* with a short 'o' (as in *hot*) rather than a long one (as in *oh*). Then there are all those words where the stress has shifted from the second syllable to the first, as with *address*, *magazine* and *research*, or the first to the second, as with *garage* and *frontier* (as in 'Space – the Final Frontier').

With *Star Trek*, *Friends*,[*] *Frasier*, *Seinfeld*, and many other

---

[*] B – Agreed, Dad. *Friends* probably did more than any other show to skew the way that people of my generation now speak English. Filmed in Los Angeles and set in New York, performed by actors from LA, Massachusetts/Canada, Alabama, LA again, Massachusetts again, and amazingly, one actually from New York City (Rachel, Chandler, Monica, Phoebe, Joey, and Ross, in that order), I've probably seen 98 per cent of the ten[**] series of *Friends* that were produced, and I've probably seen a few of those five times over. I'm aware this makes me something of a novice.

[**] B – For the record, there are 5,760 minutes of *Friends* available to watch: 10 seasons at 24 episodes per season at 24 minutes per episode. That's (not allowing for longer episodes, or DVD extras) 96 full hours, straight, without a snack-break. I'm pretty sure in 2004 I'd have recognized Matthew Perry's voice before I recognized my cousin's. Could I BE any more accommodating?

hugely successful shows following, the spread of American usages among young people was inevitable. But America doesn't explain the whole story of modern English pronunciation. In fact, by the time you get to the end of this book, you'll see that it accounts for only a small part of the extraordinary soundscape that we call 'English accents'.

INTRODUCTION: THE SOUND OF BLUE

BEN Flash forward ten years. This is how it is when you're recording a voice-over for a TV or radio commercial: you sit in a small, soundproofed booth. There's water, sometimes a hot drink. A selection of branded pens and pencils. A script, a microphone, perhaps some ambient lighting. A book stand. And a window.

Through the window, there are *lots* of people. Quite close to the window is the engineer, who usually remains silent during the session, trying not to roll his eyes. Behind the engineer, on couches, chairs, or just stalking around, are the clients, the marketing department, the director, exec producers, and the advertising company project leaders (all surrounded by magazines, fruit, biscuits, or a 'quirky' jar of sweets, and legion empty caffeine delivery devices).

You have four words printed on the script. You are the voice of a national and international advertising campaign. The four words are, 'Say hello to tomorrow'.

You are being paid to say these four words exactly as they sound in the heads of the twenty-two people staring at you on the other side of the glass. Your palms, trying not to sweat, lie flat in front of you on the green cloth* table top.

Over the last six months, perhaps a year, these four words have been whittled down from *thousands*, and They have chosen YOU to bring them to life for, despite being incredibly good at their individual jobs, they have little to no capacity to articulate the sound in their heads into words that are in any way, shape, or form, useful to another sentient being.

But it's not YOU, it's ME, and now they are all beaming those words through the glass towards me, hoping they will fly out of my mouth, through the microphone, into the recording desk and back onto the screen, where the film they have feverishly sculpted waits patiently, each frame perfectly aligned to try to persuade the general public to spend the maximum amount of money on their particular product.

Sometimes their lips move, the engineer having flicked a switch which stops the sound of their room from entering my headphones, and my knuckles whiten as I try not to let paranoia rise in my stomach: they're not talking about recasting me, they're just . . . no, they are probably trying to recast me.

A *click* in my ear.

Exec – Yeah, hi, er, Bill, sorry, Ben, ha, can you er . . . can you just forget it's *raining* outside—

– Raining?

Exec – Yeah, you sound kinda . . . sad.

---

* Baize, so when you put a pencil or glass of water down, it makes less noise. Aside from the sounds you spill into the mic, your presence must be Trappist-like.

– OK . . .

Exec – And could you say it more, er, blue.

– Blue. Like, the colour?

Another *click*. Lips. *Click.*

Exec – Yeah. Wait. Yeah! Aquamarine.

– . . .

Smile.

– Sure thing. No problem.

Engineer – Rolling. Take twelve.

Click. I hear exhalation in the word *twelve.*

The onscreen countdown starts, the film rolls, then the background sound finishes, and just before the logo pops up, I take a deep breath, and hold it – so the take doesn't have the sound of my breath in it – and—

Pause. Let me explain. There are two ways I can solve this particular problem of how, *in the next four seconds*, to turn the way that I said four words a minute ago into a completely different way for the *twelfth* time, while following the note of 'Aquamarine', *while* trying to figure out how on earth twenty-two opinions have coalesced into 'More blue'. Thanks to the somewhat passive-aggressive mention of the weather outside, I'm pretty sure they don't mean 'depressed', which worryingly means they want me to convey actual colour with the tone of my voice.

I have two main options here – three, if you count hiding under the desk.* The first is to vary the register, deepen my

---

* Which I may or may not have done during my first and only job as a lighting-board operator. I didn't know which button to press and so, from underneath the desk, blindly pressed them all, momentarily

voice maybe, think of a happy seascape – azure by white sand, wooden tables sinking into dunes – close my eyes, smile . . .

Or I could do the second, I could think of home, the coast of Wales, and bring a different _colour_* or _character_ into my voice. This naturally happens when I speak in the accent of my home, or my university county of Lancashire, or Somerset, or London, or any of the accents that, by this relatively early point in my acting career, I had mastered. I made a choice. Stuck with my natural RP accent.

Say hello to tomorrow.

I held my breath again.

Lips.

Click.

Engineer – OK, you're done.

– Yeah, we're done?

Engineer – . . . Yep.

– Great. I'll come out.

I'm so fired.

Exec – Thank you so much, perfect. Got there in the end.

---

turning the end of what had begun as a very fine production of a Pinter play into a disco.

* Rather than 'hue', _Colour_ is making a word sound like it should do. Think of the words 'majesty' and 'dustbin'. You can say both with the same vocal colour if you want, but one has a colour that shines and sparkles with gold, and the other is dusty, dull, and dirty. As an actor, you get used to making a word sound like its colour. At least, if you like being paid, you do.

– Aw! Thanks all!

Yep. Definitely didn't give them what they they wanted. I did a blocky, solid wave to the room at large – I had not been introduced to anyone when I arrived, only told to go sit in the booth – so even this desultory, soundproofed farewell seemed futile, not that anyone was looking in my direction.

For the whole of the previous year, my accent – the particular blend of place and experience that makes me – well, *me* – had been the sound of 'tomorrow'. Whatever magic these people heard in my voice fitted their work and dreams perfectly – and then, just like that, the campaign no longer suited my type of 'blue', which is the simple, cold-hearted nature of showbiz, ladles and jelly spoons.

So yeah. The next day, I totally did get fired from the gig. *C'est la vie*.

Like scones and clotted cream in Devon, or wasps in a summer London pub, accents are all around us, everywhere we go. They're among the most personal parts of ourselves that we show to the world, revealing our life history and experiences to date simply by the way we sound our speech.

In my work as an actor, voice-over artist, or producer of Shakespeare, accents come up a lot – and with a linguist father and speech-therapist mother, when I head home to North Wales it's often a tea-time conversation.* How are they used? Why do we have them?

---

* It's *always* fun-times at the Crystal residence.

Accents lie at the heart of what makes us human. We can use make-up or get plastic surgery to look different, and our choice of clothes sends an incredibly strong signal about how we'd like everyone else to perceive us. When I wear a suit, I'm businesslike; I wear jeans and a hoodie in a cafe on a Wednesday afternoon, I'm a creative; sandals and a smile on the beach (trunks too – it's not *that* sort of beach) show I'm comfortable with my body. A burqa, a kilt, tattoos, or glasses – they all tell different stories of our lives.

But an accent is a personality flag that we all fly with brighter colours than any garment, and most of us can do little to hide it. They make us who we are, and can influence the way we think – something advertising account managers, listening out for *exactly* the right shade of blue, know all too well.

The technical term for my base accent – the one I use without thinking – is 'modified RP', a slightly rougher version of Received Pronunciation, the classic 'BBC' English accent that we'll meet properly later in this book. I was born in Ascot, raised near Reading, and grew up in North Wales.* Then I went to Lancaster University, so I also have their short 'a' in my accent (I say *bath* as often as I say *baaaath*).

Then Lahndan to train as an actuh, so there's a bit o' the ol' Cockney in me pipes too. And I travel a fair bit, with a bunch of friends in the States, so my accent has a bit of a transadlandic quality to it, as I 'flap' my *t*s making them sound like *d*s. I often tell my dawg to seddle down while I boil

---

* Soo whhhenevuh ai goo hooome ai tauk a bit laik this laik.

the keddle. So my modified RP is very much a mongrel accent, which will randomly slip its leash and head off into a different part of the world.

Despite my accent being somewhat autonomous, it's mine and I'm fiercely protective of it. It's me. Once – and only once – I made the foolish mistake of correcting someone, a girl, my girlfriend, on the way she pronounced something* – it's as personal a comment as any I know.

I remember it beginning to change into this accent mish-mash. I'm aware that at some point in my twenties I started saying *conCRETE*, instead of the British *CONcrete*, and some-times, yes, even *adverTISEment* instead of *adVERtisement* – a litmus test if ever there was one of which side of the Atlantic you were raised, sorry, brought up.

Back in the nineteenth century it was the absolute norm to talk about the thing Juliet looks out from, and Romeo tries to climb, as a

bal-COH-ny

and some people hated the fact that there were IDIOTS who would pronounce it

BAL-con-y

but eventually the standard pronunciation changed. Such knee-jerk judgements of others form a big part of what this book is about. These vocal-melodic shifts or changes in stress patterns occur all the time. As groups of people splinter and travel to different land masses, a change slowly rumbles to

---

* OK, yes, EX-girlfriend.

the surface of common usage as they attempt to demonstrate their individuality from their country of origin. Judgement of how they sound is a natural follow-on.

But while this book looks at what our accents say about us – and what they say about others – it is also a geographical tour through the English-speaking world, and a journey back in time to learn more about *why* we speak the way we do.

We'll look at what accents have to say about social status, and the rise of 'Received Pronunciation' – the 'posh', stereotypically British accent.

We'll look at how Shakespeare might have actually pronounced the lines from his own plays, and share some of the excitement of producing his work in OP – Original Pronunciation – for the first time in centuries.

And we'll also look at the increasing dominance of American English, and the question of whether our beloved local accents will eventually die out.

But before we get there, we need to confront the elephant in the room and set down what an accent actually *is*. And for that, I need m'father, Professor David Crystal. This book is about accents, and while accents do form a large part of my *art*, this is Dad's *craft*.

Over to you, Pops.

QUESTION: WHAT IS AN ACCENT?

DAVID As Ben's suggested, the heart of the answer is the notion that accents express our identity – who we are, which part of the country we come from, or where we belong socially or professionally. And identity is a very emotional issue.

We need to be clear what we're talking about, when we refer to someone's 'accent'. Accents have to be distinguished from dialects. An accent is a person's distinctive pronunciation. A dialect is a much broader notion: it refers to the distinctive vocabulary and grammar of someone's use of language. If you say *eether* and I say *iyther*, that's accent. We use the same word but pronounce it differently. But if you say *I've got a new dustbin* and I say *I've gotten a new garbage can*, that's dialect. We're using different words and sentence patterns to talk about the same thing. This book is just about accents.

Usually, when people talk about accents, they're thinking geographically. A pronunciation shows you come from a particular part of a country, or – in the case of English, now used all over the world – from a particular country. If you pronounce the first syllable of *lieutenant* as 'loo', you're American – or come from a part of the world influenced by American English. If you pronounce it like 'left', you're British, or British-influenced – which is why it's 'left-' in Australia and Canada.

But often an accent does more than point to a region. It tells you about a person's social background – the social class they belong to, or their educational history, or their ethnic or religious affiliation. If we were to explore the personal histories of Ben and someone else, that girl, his ex-girlfriend, we'd find social factors in the way they were brought up that account for their different preferences. Most people remember having some feature of their pronunciation corrected by their parents, or by a teacher in school. As adults, some go out of their way to change their accent, because they want to sound like people from a social class they aspire to.

There's a third function of accent: it can tell you what job a person does. Listen to lawyers and judges talking in court, or ministers giving a sermon, or drill sergeants haranguing their squads, or football commentators describing a game, and you're hearing occupational accents. These professionals don't talk in that way when they're off-duty. A household resounding to the excited tones of 'You 'orrible little man!' or 'They think it's all over!' would be an unusual place indeed.

And we mustn't forget the individual function of accent: it can convey our personal identity to the rest of the world. This is the recognition factor. We recognize someone we know from their voice. It might be a family member, a neighbour, a public figure, or a personality on radio or television. We can do this because no two people have exactly the same accent and voice quality.

The sound of our voice is produced by the configuration of the organs in our vocal tract. The shape of our tongue, the height of our palate, the thickness of our vocal cords, the size of our nose, the width of our windpipe, the contour of our lips . . . all of this results in a personal anatomical architecture that is unique. There are as many accents in a language as there are people who speak it. Everyone has an accent. It's like fingerprints, but on a grander scale.

In the beginning . . .

Why is there such extraordinary diversity? Why don't we all have the same accent? There's a reason for everything, evolutionary biologists say. And if we think of accents and identity in terms of evolution, a reason for accent variation does emerge.

Let's think further about Ben's list of ways in which we express our identity, from burqas to beachwear. There are so many things we can do to show we belong in a particular group, from the clothes we wear to the national flags we wave at the Olympics. We can sport a badge that tells the rest of the world who we are. And we can do something that is different from all these things: we can speak with a particular accent.

What's the difference? We have to go out of our way to find clothes, flags, banners, and badges, spending both time and money. Accents, on the other hand, grow up with us from an early age, naturally and unconsciously. And they cost nothing at all.

In addition, clothes, flags, banners, and badges have some serious limitations as markers of identity. They can't be seen around corners, and they can't be seen in the dark. The human voice doesn't have these problems. It can be perceived both around corners and in the dark. It is the only all-inclusive means of expressing identity that we have.

Perceiving identities in the dark would have been a critical factor in the early development of the human race, when speech was emerging for the first time. Imagine you're in a cave, and you hear voices outside. Are they friends or enemies? You call out. A voice replies. If the voice has the same accent as yours, it's probably safe to go outside, as the speaker is a member of your tribe. If the voice has a different accent, you can still go outside, but you'd better take your club with you! That is one way of thinking about accents – as a linguistic dimension to the survival of the fittest.

Fast forward a hundred thousand years or so, and things haven't changed all that much. I remember a conversation I had with a streetwise young man some years ago who told me he knew not to round a corner into a street, or go into a club or pub, if he heard a particular accent being used there. Often that accent was ethnic in origin. Conversely, he could recognize 'friendly' accents at a distance, ethnic or otherwise. In a society where different groups don't get on, listening to accents can still be a matter of survival.

Before we're born

Our ability to distinguish voices is something deeply ingrained in human nature. It's actually there before we are born. From around thirty weeks after conception, the ears of the foetus are sufficiently well formed to enable it to hear what is going on. The tiny little bones inside our ears, which transmit sound to our brain, are already fully developed by the time we're born.

During some types of gynaecological examination, researchers have inserted a tiny microphone, called a hydrophone, into the uterus, enabling them to hear what the foetus can hear. And what the foetus hears is a great deal of background noise – the mother's heartbeat, the blood sloshing around the arteries, tummy and intestine rumbles, voices and loud noises from outside – and, above all, the mother's voice resonating through her tissues, bones, and fluids. The foetus is asleep a lot of the time, but when awake, its heart rate slows when the mother is speaking – the first sign of a calming response.

It can't hear everything perfectly, of course. The effect is a bit like listening to someone talking with cotton wool in our ears. The voice sounds distant and muffled. But there are certain things the foetus can hear very clearly. It can hear the intonation, or melody, of the mother's voice, and it can hear the loudness and rhythm of her speech – and that includes her accent. Sound and movement combine: when she laughs, the foetus can be seen to bounce around.

Once the baby is born, researchers have performed experiments to demonstrate just how much the foetus has heard. They monitor the baby's heart rate, the constitution of its saliva, the way it turns its head, the length of time it looks in a certain direction, or the rate at which it sucks on a special kind of nipple. The idea is that if a baby recognizes something, or is especially interested in something, then its heart rate or saliva content will alter, or it will turn its head towards a stimulus, or it will look at a stimulus for longer, or it will suck faster.

This is the sort of thing they've found. Newborn babies, even just a day old, prefer their mother's voice to that of a stranger. They show more interest when hearing their native language as opposed to a foreign language. If the mother has told the foetus a particular story during her pregnancy, the baby shows a preference to that compared with an unfamiliar story. And the effect of music emerges too – an important finding for accents, as the character of an accent owes much to its melodic lilt.

One study played the same tune to a group of mothers every day throughout pregnancy; another group of mothers didn't hear the tune. When all the babies were born, the tune was played to them. The changes in heart rate, movement, and general alertness of the 'musical' babies showed clearly that they recognized the tune. To check that it wasn't just a general response to music, the researchers played the babies a different tune, but they didn't react to it. Nor did they react to it when they heard the same tune played backwards! There seems to be something special about the music of the voice. From the moment the baby is born, the mother – and other caretakers too – start talking to the baby in an unusual way. We call it 'baby talk'. One of its most noticeable features is the way the voice ascends and descends throughout its whole pitch range – almost like singing in speech. And the exaggerated tones stay throughout the first year of life. The mother's voice is higher in pitch, and she speaks more slowly, when addressing her baby than when talking to others, and she's emotionally much more expressive. The effects can be clearly heard when playing simple games, such as peep-bo (peek-a-boo) or round-and-round-the-garden.

Not surprisingly, then, the first features of the mother's language that the baby learns to reproduce are its intonation and rhythm. If we record babies' early vocalizations, at around a month or so of age, we can't tell which language they're learning. Nor can we tell from their cooing or babbling. But at around nine months the vocalizations start to sound 'shaped', and it's possible to distinguish babies who are learning English from those learning French from those learning Chinese, and so on. This is long before they learn any words, so what is it that we notice? The rhythm and intonation of the languages. The English baby is vocalizing with a 'tum-te-tum' rhythm. The French baby with a 'rat-a-tat-a-tat' rhythm. The Chinese baby with a sing-song rhythm. Why intonation and rhythm? It's no coincidence that these were the very features first perceived in the womb.

Melody, whether of speech or music, seems to be especially significant when talking about accents. Think of some of the accents you know, and try to describe them. It's quite difficult to talk about the distinctive vowels and consonants they use; it's much easier to say something about their musical properties. We describe their pitch, loudness, speed, and rhythm, just as we do with music. We say one accent is higher or slower than another, or it has a rising lilt. We talk about a drawling accent or a nasal twang. In *The Muppets*, everyone recognized the Swedish chef, not because of his words (which were unintelligible), but because of the Swedish melody of his speech.

Accents emerge in children's speech as soon as they're capable of producing words, which for most is around the end of the first year of life. The difference in vowel quality between an American *mommy* and a British *mummy* or *mama* can be heard very early on. And when words like *there* and *more* begin to be used, that final *–r* will be heard if it's in the parents' accent. By age two, a child has an accent that sounds like the one used by its parents and siblings. More than one accent, in the case of children growing up bilingually.

The process continues. Most parents have had the experience of listening to their three-year-old chattering away while playing with toys and suddenly hearing their own tones of voice when their little one gives a doll or a toy animal a sharp telling off. And when a child 'leaves home' for the first time, and starts to play with other children in a crèche or nursery, one of the first things parents notice is a new pronunciation brought home from the crèche. Indeed, the child need not even leave home to pick up a 'foreign' accent. If a family makes regular use of a home help with a different accent, the influence will be there.

One of the most fascinating things about this whole process is that children 'know' who they're talking to, and adapt their pronunciation accordingly. This happens even in the first year of life, before real language starts. A child babbling away to its mother does so with a higher pitch range than when babbling away to its father. Children seem to instinctively sense the chief features of the voice they're interacting with, and copy them – or *accommodate* to them, as linguists say. It's an ability that will stay with them for the rest of their lives, and we'll see some of the consequences later in this book.

How we make sounds

When we speak, we use all parts of our vocal tract, as shown below.

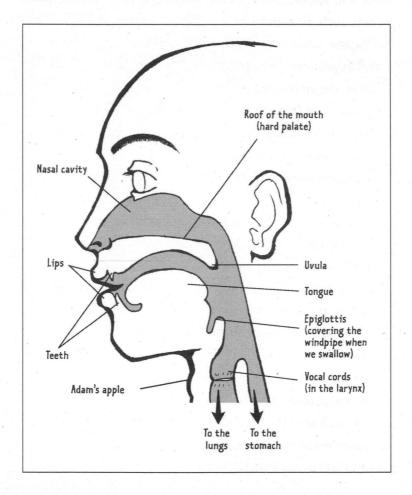

Air from the lungs comes up our windpipe and passes the vocal cords, situated in the larynx (behind our Adam's apple). If nothing impedes the air, out it comes in the form of an *h*. If the air makes the vocal cords vibrate, they produce the 'buzz' that we hear when we make such consonants as *b*, *z*, and *m*. These are called *voiced* sounds. You can hear the contrast between *voiced* and *voiceless* most clearly if you compare pairs of consonants such as *z* and *s* or *v* and *f*, which are articulated in exactly the same way – apart from that buzzing. Put your fingers in your ears to hear the contrast most clearly.

When the air reaches the back of the throat, it can go in two directions – out through the mouth or out through the nose. If we speak while the air is coming out through the nose, we produce a *nasal* effect – an important feature of some accents. Three English consonants rely on the nose for their effect: *m*, *n*, and *ng*.

If the air goes out through the mouth, the sound is immediately shaped by the movement of the tongue. This produces many of the consonants and all of the vowels (see below).

Finally, the air passes through the teeth and lips. It can be blocked at the teeth, as when we make the two *th* sounds (voiceless in *thin*, voiced in *this*). And it can be blocked, or partially blocked, at the lips (as in *p*, *b*, *m*), or with the bottom lip against the top teeth (as in *f* and *v*).

The vocal cords are also involved in the way we vary our pitch, as well as in the production of various other vocal effects (such as when we speak loudly or softly, or in a breathy way). The rises and falls in voice pitch (our *intonation*) are a very important feature distinguishing accents. Accents may also vary in the way they place the loudness (the *stress*) in a word.

Not shown in the diagram is the way we can speak faster or slower, or vary our rhythm. Different speeds and rhythms can distinguish accents too.

Consonants

These are made in several ways.

- The tongue or lips can block the sound completely – as when we say *p, b, m, t, d, n, k, g, ng*.

- The tongue produces an audible friction by moving close to the roof of the mouth or the teeth - as when we say *s, z, sh, zh* (as in *confusion*), *ch, dg* (as in *judge*), *h*, and the two *th* sounds (*thin, this*). In the case of *f* and *v*, the friction is caused by lip against teeth.

- The tongue allows air around the sides of the tongue, as when we say *l* - you can feel this effect if, while making an *l* sound, you breathe in suddenly. You'll feel the air rushing around both sides of your mouth. If the front of the tongue is raised towards the roof of the mouth, the result is a 'clear *l*' (as in *leap*); if it dips, so that the back is high, the result is a 'dark *l*' (as in *peel*).

- The tip of the tongue comes close to the ridge behind the top teeth, to make the *r* sound in words like *red*. Sometimes it flaps, in words like *very*. With some accents, the tip of the tongue curls backwards to make a much darker 'retroflex' *r* sound. With others, the tip vibrates against the teeth ridge, to make a trilled *r*. Sometimes the very back of the tongue vibrates against the uvula. Sounding the *r* after a vowel, as a retroflex or trill, is a very common feature of English accents.

- Two consonants, *w* (as in *Wales*) and *y* (as in *yes*) actually sound like very short versions of the vowels 'oo' and 'ee'. Some accents have a voiceless *w*, thus distinguishing *Wales* and *whales*.

Vowels

Most of the distinctiveness of English accents comes from the vowels. There are three main types.

- *Pure vowels* have a single auditory quality. Say 'ah' (as at the doctor's) and keep it going. It has the same quality throughout.

- *Diphthongs* have two auditory qualities. The tongue starts with one position in the mouth and quickly moves to another. Say *my* slowly, and you'll feel (and hear) the tongue start in a mouth-open position and move up towards the roof of the mouth.

- *Triphthongs* have three auditory qualities. Say *fire* as 'fie-yuh' and you'll sense the first part doing the same thing as in *my* above, but followed by an 'uh' ending in the centre of the mouth. (If you normally say *fire* as 'fah', you'll have to work at this one.)

- Some pure vowels are short: *pit, pet, pat, putt, pot, put,* and the vowel in unstressed *the.* Some accents have longer versions of these vowels, and some turn them into diphthongs.

- Some pure vowels are long: *see, palm, soon, thought, nurse.* Some accents have shorter versions of these vowels, and some turn them into diphthongs.

- And here are the diphthongs: *aim, my, oil, goat, owl, ear, air, your.* Some accents turn these diphthongs into pure vowels (such as 'ahl' for *oil*).

When these vowels are made with the front of the tongue, we say they are 'front' vowels (as in *see, pit, pet, pat*). Other vowels are made further back in the mouth: 'central' vowels (*putt, the, nurse*), and 'back vowels' (*pot, put, palm, thought, soon*).

Some vowels (such as *pit* and *see*) are made with the tongue higher in the mouth; some (such as *pat* and *palm*) with it lower. We can then describe accents as 'raising' or 'lowering' a vowel compared with other accents.

Some vowels have the lips rounded; others have the lips spread. Compare *pot* and *put* with the other short vowels, or *soon* and *thought* with the other long vowels. Accents vary in how much lip-rounding they use.

All this makes an inventory of twenty-four consonants and twenty vowels. As a slight change in any one of these in combination with any other can be the basis of a distinctive accent, it's clear that the accent possibilities in English are virtually endless.

The amazing thing is that we have the ability to tune in to these slight differences, and make the kinds of judgements about identity that we discuss in this book.

PART ONE

ACCENT PASSIONS

ACCENT BUDDIES

BEN When we're young, and first begin experimenting with expressing our opinions, we're like over-enthusiastic children learning to skip stones. Nervous and new-found knowledge is hurled like a rock into conversational pools, soaking everyone. But these are the risks and mistakes we have to take as we, both literally and metaphorically, find our voice.

Rarely, as children, are we required to sculpt the type of sound we make; parents are usually overjoyed that language is being acquired at all; who cares what accent it's in? Gaining control over the flips and tricks your voice box can accomplish in tandem with a mouth of tongue and bones to create the spoken word – let alone song – is no small feat.

Adapting those flips and slips to create slightly *different* sounds, ones that don't belong to your lifetime's experiences and upbringing to date, is hard for most, considered impossible for some, and a talent a lucky few can make an entire career out of.

Now, not all actors are good with accents. Some people can play five instruments, or dance, or horse-ride, and some can do every English accent there is. Drama schools encourage actors to learn how to adopt other accents, whether it be by ear (listening to the sound over and over) or by eye (learning and reading the sound alphabet linguists have devised, the International Phonetic Alphabet*).

The first time I noticed my accent markedly shift was when drunk in university. My accent began to gently mirror those of my new friends – I experienced the *accommodation* Dad's just talked about (distinct from the prison-cell university housing we were given) – a psycholinguistic subconscious trait we all manifest. I will sound a bit more like you, and you will sound a bit more like me, and it is the accent way of saying, 'We are buddies.'

Accent buddies. Think of teenage boys wanting to sound like deep-voiced, smooth-talking men, or pop stars from Mick Jagger to Adele ditching their accents while singing in favour of the all-conquering – and globally encountered – American variant.

You notice accommodation in strangers from another land, now satirized beyond redemption in the British *Carry On* films and the TV programme from the 1980s, *'Allo 'Allo*. Upon noticing that an enquirer of directions is a learner of your language, a set of manoeuvres is activated, namely, a slowing down of speech to the point where our map-holding

---

* The IPA is essentially a mouth alphabet – vowels and consonant sounds are located in a particular part of the mouth – but you'll notice that in this book, we're using a much simpler sound-a-like way of writing down a pro-nun-see-EH-shun. Why? (1) I don't think it's especially necessary to learn the IPA for a few words here and there, and (2) I've forgotten most of it, much to Dad's chagrin.

friend thinks you've gone into slo-mo, and for some reason you acquire the gestural subtlety of a drunken giraffe.

At the same time as the arms are flailing, and a passer-by could be forgiven for thinking you're directing an aeroplane to its gate, difficult words are avoided, and the accents of both speakers soften.

It's funny, though, how your voice – the sound you hear when you speak and the one you might wish to change – is not the same sound you hear when you listen back to a voicemail you've left.

We hear our spoken voice partly with our ears through the air, but mostly the sound travels through the bones in our face. That small journey makes my already fairly deep voice sound much deeper to me. 'I hate hearing myself recorded' is the catchphrase, because we're so unused to hearing it the way others do. Our voices will always sound utterly different to us, a personal sound that no one else will ever hear.

When I write, my voice inside my head sounds out the words I type. Then I silently read back what I've written, and assuming it isn't complete garbage, go back and, having corrected for my tendency to over-add commas, make sure it sounds 'right'.

The other 'sound' that most people hear in their heads comes when they're silently reading a novel. We can project other people's accents onto the words we read, if we've heard them often enough, be they a parent, an ex-lover, Marilyn Monroe or Stephen Fry. It's a neat trick – and it tells us something about how accents lie at the very heart of human interaction.

We are stunningly quick to come to a conclusion about

a voice we hear – the friend or enemy outside the cave. There's nothing special or unique about English – a series of idiosyncratic sounds made by smacking bone against flesh and pushing air around like any language – but we will often make statements about someone's economic or educational background from the sound of their voice alone, without knowing a single thing about them.

In a photograph or on a Twitter feed I could be anyone; but with my accent, I can and will be immediately labelled, whether that label be 'posh', 'common', 'stupid', 'educated', or 'foreign'. Such labelling leads people to try to change their accent, either to encourage such associations or to step further away from them.

Some do it more consciously than others. I sometimes start finding a character I'm going to play by exploring what voice they might have, like Carl Reiner's Saul, in *Ocean's Eleven* (2001).*

Young actors are told (still to this day) that they must learn RP if they want to be paid to act Shakespeare; that the Edinburgh brogue is beautiful,† Glasgow unintelligible, and Yorkshire homely – but that only RP is *proper*.

---

* Laurence Olivier, the great Shakespearean actor of the twentieth century, was famous for first getting into character from a physical standpoint, exploring how it might be to *feel* like the character in the play, their walk, their heft. But each to his own.

† These places are home to vastly different sound systems, and so when I say the Edinburgh brogue, it's really a place-holder – not everyone in the city of Edinburgh sounds the same – accents change from one side of a city to another, from one street corner to another, even house

Society is now saddled with the idea that particular accents belong to particular settings, that somehow some things sound *wrong* in a particular accent, or perhaps, more specifically, that some accents aren't the correct way of presenting a particular art form. I've met young actors across the United States, Europe and India who face the same issue: they don't feel like they have ownership or the right to speak Shakespeare because they're told they don't sound 'right'. In all my travels working on making Shakespeare more access-ible to people, the problem is never one of comprehension, it's one of permission.

The idea of speaking Shakespeare in a regional accent is, in 2014, still considered fairly experimental, so only a select few sound like they're doing it 'right'. If you haven't encoun-tered such a thing, there's something a bit special about hearing Hamlet's 'To be, or not to be' speech in Welsh, Irish, or Yorkshire. And anyway, how can someone's accent be 'wrong'?

Think of a person's accent: that personal collection of micro-sounds used to activate their dialect (the grammar and vocabulary peculiar to their neighbourhood, whose sole function is to communicate with all the other sentient monkeys nearby), forming clusters of snowflake-unique sounds, each collection as different as the next. And while each person's accent is unique, those snowflakes combined share enough

---

to house. But all speakers would share very similar elements of prosody: the musicality of an Edinburgh accent, the nasal element to Birming-ham, the cut-glass crisp articulation of RP, and so on.

similarity with the other accents nearby to clearly, vocally, mark our territory to others.

So often someone will say, 'Oh but you don't have an accent,' and even after years of living abroad people will be told they still sound 'foreign' to the locals, only to return home to the news that their accent sounds completely different. For the most part the speaker is oblivious of this slow, steady transformation, unaware of their accommodation to new acoustic surroundings.

The Australian landlady who runs the pub opposite where I live just told me the same thing. When she goes home her friends laugh at her for sounding like a posh Pom. When she's here, people ask her where her cork hat is.

Jo – And, tell your readers I've lived here fifteen years!

– I just have. So, does your accent change when you go home, then?

Jo – Aw yeah, dependin' who I talk to tho'. Most of the time I don't even notice it, tho', y'kno'?

In London, you'll blur past four hundred languages, and countless shades of spoken English, each as singular as a strand of DNA. The majority of Londoners have a language of home, a language with friends, and a language of work, or public domain – and then also speak English. So in this immense metropolis today it's more common to hear a lilt to spoken English, and often perhaps with it a feeling in the speaker of not 'sounding English enough'.

Suddenly we're into the realms of second-language learners needing an accent that makes them sound as English as possible, and of an accent's transformation from a marker of personal identity into a disguise to *gain* a cloak of invisibility within a nation.

Learning and speaking a second, third or fourth language proficiently isn't enough, it seems, because, despite this multicultural richness of London, people think they'll never sound 'fully English' unless all traces of origin are wiped. We flatten out our sense of identity to fit in, and bring out a Disney-esque, omni-cultural sound in our throats – as identity-less as a uniform or an off-the-peg office suit.

But from the micro to the global scale, this is what we all naturally do. Just as we switch dialects from home to work, our accents, chameleon-like, change with our interlocutor. Barman to bank manager, Glaswegian to Cornishman, American to Hindu, Australian to Japanese, the accent equivalent of a favourite cardigan and slippers is swapped for a pinstripe suit and brogues.

On that micro level, just as no two clarinettists sound the same, we as speakers of English are singular composers and players of speech – actors of the lines and playwrights plucking them from the air. We're able to master a variety of sounds to communicate incredibly complex thoughts, each as completely *you* as the physiology which forms them.

In theory, then, the dislike of a sound should be governed only by a dislike of the person making it, shouldn't it?

But if that *is* the case, then what on earth went wrong in Birmingham?

WHAT WENT WRONG IN BIRMINGHAM?

DAVID   There are always two sides to accents: the accents themselves, and our attitudes to them. It's the same with anything: we like it or we don't, whether it's a car design, a cooking recipe, a political party, or a work of art. Some people may not have strong views – or any views at all – about one or other of these. But when it comes to language, everyone has a like or dislike. We have views about the style of a particular poem, play, or novel. We have views about the speech we hear on radio and television. Very strong views, often. And views about accents are among the most strongly expressed of all.

It's the dislike that causes people to sound off, usually by sending a letter or email to a newspaper or a broadcasting company. In December 2013 a correspondent wrote to the *Sunday Times* about one TV presenter:

> Genuine accents are fine, but the zeal with which the BBC encourages its presenters to adopt a faux northern inflection in their speech is, at best, irritating and, at worst, disgraceful.

A week later there was a response in even more intemperate language. I imagine the editor wasn't able to print the worst ones.

I know there are worse ones because, during the 1980s, I used to present a series on BBC Radio 4 called *English Now*. Each week the BBC would send me all the letters that had come in from listeners on the subject of language – most of them complaining about something or other. It was rare indeed to see a letter of praise. Accents were always the topic that attracted most of the ire, and the words used to express the writer's attitude were always of the most extreme kind. Correspondents would say they were 'appalled', 'outraged', 'horrified', 'disgusted' . . . to hear a particular accent or a particular pronunciation (more on the genesis of this listener-horror in a little while).

It made me wonder: if words like these are being used to describe something as routine as a disliked pronunciation, what words are left in the language to describe an event of truly horrendous proportions, such as the catastrophic results of a suicide bomb?

But the modern writers are doing nothing new. Complaining about the perceived ugliness of someone else's speech is probably as old as language itself. Records are sparse, but from the early Middle Ages in Britain we find examples of uncomplimentary remarks about one accent or another. Usually, it's the south being rude about the north – as when William of Malmesbury writes in the eleventh century about Northumbria at the beginning of Book Three in his *Deeds of the Bishops of England*:

> The whole speech of the Northumbrians, especially that of the men of York, grates so harshly upon the ear that it is completely unintelligible to us Southerners.

He goes on to explain why this is:

> The reason for this is their proximity to barbaric tribes and their distance from the kings of the land, who, whether English as once or Norman as now, are known to stay more often in the south than the north.

The barbaric tribes may have long gone, but the south of England remains the hub of courtly presence.

It's no coincidence that William singles out York. City-dwellers from the north have traditionally attracted the worst criticisms, whether they be living in Glasgow, Newcastle, Manchester, or Liverpool. And 'north', it must be remembered, from a southern perspective starts somewhere around Oxford and Cambridge. So Birmingham is included in this mix – as well as places further west, such as Cardiff. But Birmingham is special.

Brummie

The Birmingham accent – Brummie, as it's usually called – has had more than its fair share of bad press. *The Times* in 1997 reported the results of a paper given to the British Psychological Society's criminal conference that year under the headline, 'Brummie accent "sounds guilty"'.

Over a hundred students picked at random were asked to listen to male actors reproducing police interviews, in which the suspects were under suspicion of either cheque fraud or armed robbery. The actors gave each suspect either a Birmingham accent or Received Pronunciation, and the students had to say whether the suspects were guilty or innocent based only on their judgement of the voices. The members of the student 'jury' were twice as likely to convict a suspect who had a Brummie accent. Moreover, there was no difference between the crimes. Regardless of whether you were a white-collar cheque fraudster or a blue-collar armed robber, a Brummie accent could send you down.

A *Times* editorial expressed its horror at the outcome. It headed its piece, 'Accent is as useless an indicator of guilt as colour of hair'. And it ended, 'a crook's a crook for a' that, however received or unreceived his pronunciation'. There's certainly a movie truth in that. As we discuss later, anyone who watches Hollywood movies knows that an upper-crust English accent is the sure sign of a villain. But within Britain, things are evidently different, and a remarkable anti-Brummie prejudice rules.

A decade on from the 1997 study, not much had changed. In 2005 the BBC carried out a survey as part of its *Voices* project – an unprecedented celebration on radio and television of accents and dialects in the UK. It ranked thirty-four accents in terms of pleasantness, prestige, and career helpfulness. At the top, each time, came the standard accent of England, Received Pronunciation. And at the bottom, each time, Birmingham.

It isn't just associations of ugliness and criminality. If you ask people to rate accents in terms of laziness, stupidity, bolshiness, and other negative values, Brummie persistently comes out low, though not always bottom. Brummies can take some comfort that they are outranked for bolshiness by Northern Ireland, doubtless due to the threatening tones of voice associated with vocal hardline fundamentalism during the worst of the Troubles.

In 2008 a study of perceived intelligence reached the same dismal conclusion. Researchers asked forty-eight volunteers to look at photos of female models while listening to recordings of women with different accents – Yorkshire, Received Pronunciation, and Birmingham – or with no voice-over at all. They were then asked to rate the models for intelligence, giving them marks out of ten. Yorkshire came top, with 6.71, just beating RP with 6.67 (a remarkable result in itself, which I'll talk about later). Then came silence, with 5.99. And Birmingham came bottom with 5.6.

Before I go any further, let me affirm as loudly as I can that there is, of course, no correlation whatsoever between the sound of a language or dialect and the level of intelligence or sociability of its speakers. The only reason we might think otherwise is because for generations people were told so by their – for want of a better word – 'betters'. Traditionally, the English aristocracy looked down on provincial speech, considering it harsh and rough. Nobles who had received a good education would naturally think of provincials as ignorant and lazy, and associate their lack of knowledge with the way they talked. It's then a short step from saying that people are ignorant to saying that they're unintelligent.

A classic example is John Walker, who wrote the first *English Pronouncing Dictionary* at the end of the eighteenth century. In his subtitle he tells his readers that one of his aims is to give 'Rules to be Observed by the Natives of Scotland, Ireland, and London, for Avoiding their Respective Peculiarities'. He's in no doubt that they are in desperate need of help. He ends his section on London with the observation:

> the vulgar pronunciation of London, though not half so erroneous as that of Scotland, Ireland, or any of the provinces, is, to a person of correct taste, a thousand times more offensive and disgusting.

At least he doesn't single Birmingham out for special attention.

What is it about Birmingham? In today's more egalitarian age, crude stereotypes about social class and intelligence are no longer in fashion. Other city accents have had improved ratings. As we'll see later on, these days regional city accents are much more likely to be perceived as warm, kind, and customer-friendly. A well-known and popular personality can single-handedly improve the ratings of a city accent. Think Billy Connolly and Glasgow. Or a group of personalities. Think Beatles and Liverpool. But the Birmingham stereotype has remained.

A clue comes from a different experiment. If you play a set of English accents to foreigners who can't speak English, or who aren't familiar with British social history, and ask them to rate the accents in terms of their beauty or ugliness, you'd be surprised at some of the results. Birmingham actually comes out top of the beauty scale for many listeners. When I played some Brummie tapes to a group of foreigners at a summer school, they described the accent as 'melodious' and 'musical'.

In 1998, Gary Finn in the *Independent* reported that 'In Israeli clubs the sexiest sounds are Midland vowels'. It transpired that a nightclub owner in Haifa had advertised in Birmingham's *Sunday Mercury* for staff to come and work in his club during the winter months. The owner said, 'I love the accent, and nightclub-goers can't get enough of it over here. I believe you can go a long way if you can speak the Birmingham way.' And he concludes, 'I've heard enough holiday-makers from the region to know it's the best accent by far.'

Comments like these suggest that what people are reacting to is not so much the acoustic qualities of the accent as the psychological associations that the accent has accreted over the years. Where did these associations come from? The outcome of the BBC's *Voices* project was a whole week of national and local programmes in August 2005. One, made by West Midlands radio, and called *Was It Something We Said?*, investigated the local linguistic situation. The contributors were quite clear about the origins of the negative stereotype. Birmingham was the prime example of the nineteenth-century dirty and sprawling city, and it was inevitable that the association of 'ugly city' would carry over into 'ugly speech'.

There's a story that Queen Victoria pulled down the blinds on the windows of the royal train as she travelled from Birmingham to Wolverhampton. It's probably only a legend, but truth is never a factor in the creation of stereotypes. And the name of the region to the north of Birmingham, the 'Black Country', doesn't help. The adjective probably derives from the huge coal seam that underlies the area, the richest in Britain; but it's the black smoke and soot of the industrial chimneys that people remember when they hear it. Today the arca is far more green than black. The bright and spacious regenerated Birmingham city centre has begun to eat away at the old stereotype. But it is much easier to regenerate a city than an accent, especially one like Birmingham's, which – if you are so inclined – is so easy to mock.

Brummie is an interesting accent, a blend of northern and southern features, slightly nasal, strongly velar (towards the back of the mouth), with lengthened vowels. It has a slow rate of articulation and a somewhat sing-song intonation. A slow delivery is much easier to exaggerate than a fast one, so it's not surprising to hear it often caricatured on radio and television.

Needless to say, the exaggerated versions you hear from comedians bear little relationship to the accents that are actually used on the streets. And note – *accents*. There are huge differences between the way they speak in different parts of the Black Country. Locals can tell people apart within just a few miles. Birmingham speech is not at all like the speech of Dudley or Wolverhampton. But, to the media comic who wants a cheap laugh, they're all the same.

Why the stupidity?

The industrial history of the city might explain the sense of ugliness, but why the stupidity? Here we have to look for individual influences. Ask older people who they associate with the Birmingham accent and they'll usually remember the comedienne Beryl Reid, who portrayed the character of Marlene, the Pride of the Midlands, in the radio show *Educating Archie* in the 1950s. She was known for her enormous earrings, her catchphrases, and her hugely exaggerated Brummie accent: 'Good evening, each. My name's Marlene' – and when talking about one of her boyfriends: 'He's terriffeec. He sends me.' Marlene wasn't the brightest of individuals. The whole nation heard it, believed it, and generalized it to the entire Birmingham community.

It's difficult now to imagine the force of radio in a pre-television age. *Educating Archie* was so successful that it ran for a decade, winning several variety awards – a remarkable achievement for a show where the leading characters were a ventriloquist (Peter Brough) and his dummy (Archie). A ventriloquist on the radio. Think about it.

The myth of people from the Midlands being a bit slow was reinforced by other characters from other series, such as the simple-minded handyman, Benny Hawkins, from the ITV television soap *Crossroads* – though his Midlands accent was very mild and gentle compared to Marlene's raucous voice – and the bumblingly innocent electrician, Barry Taylor, from the BBC's *Auf Wiedersehen, Pet*. The accent spread around the stand-up comedy circuit. Comedians such as Jasper Carrott sensed the comic power of having an accent that could, it appeared, express special stupidity. He even transferred it into song, with the mock-biker anthem 'Funky Moped', a top-ten hit in 1975 ('roide, roide, roide . . .'). There's nothing unique about this. Most nations have a part of the country where the people are thought to be mentally slower than everywhere else. Usually it's in a remote corner of the land, well away from the capital. It's a bit unusual to encounter it in the centre of a country, as with Birmingham, and unique, I think, to see it in relation to a country's second largest city.

The presenter of *Was It Something We Said?* concluded that London was frightened of Birmingham, and that there has been a long-standing southern prejudice against the wealth-creators of the Midlands. Londoners have a vested interest, so the argument went, in keeping Birmingham down. And what better way to do that than to foster stereotypes that the people of Birmingham are lazy and thick, and to use their accent as a means to that end?

The stereotype has carried over into the theatre. In Stratford in 2005 there was a splendid production of *A Midsummer Night's Dream* by the Royal Shakespeare Company, directed by Gregory Doran. Bottom and the other rustics presented us with some side-splitting moments. But they had all adopted Brummie accents. This gave the opportunity for a number of cheap laughs – though not from me. Theatre companies above all should be trying to break down stereotypes, not fostering them.

It will take national characters with a totally positive

image to reverse the situation for Birmingham. It hasn't happened yet. People with the accent are still scared of it, and go out of their way to change it as they plan their careers. I can think of hardly any media or theatre personalities from the Midlands who have kept their home accent. Some took elocution lessons to eliminate it. We don't think of Birmingham when we hear comedian Tony Hancock, broadcaster Sue Lawley, novelist Barbara Cartland, or actress Julie Walters. But they were all brought up in the Midlands.

Things will change only if more positive role models become known through radio and television. The media have the primary responsibility, as we'll see with the successful cases I'll talk about later. The South Wales accent was another that traditionally had a bad press. During the 1983 general election campaign, pundits often commented on Labour leader Neil Kinnock's South Wales accent as a factor in his losing the election. But television newsreader Huw Edwards has been influential in altering public perception. People now often describe his accent as 'authoritative' and 'thoughtful' – a direct reflection of his broadcasting role. And it has happened within a generation.

The same thing could happen to Brummie too. Attitudes are slowly changing, helped by an evolving cultural climate which attacks negative stereotypes about social groups. *The Times* editorial agreed:

Brum was once the accent of Shakespeare and Dr Johnson, of the steelmasters of the Industrial Revolution and the Chamberlains. So it was not always at the bottom of the English Tower of Babel. And it need not stay there. What Birmingham needs to give its accent prestige is a pop group such as the Beatles or Oasis, or a new soap opera such as *Neighbours*.

And for a few moments, in 2013, I thought this was going to happen.

My optimism came from the publicity preceding a new BBC gangster series, *Peaky Blinders*, set in Birmingham just after World War I, when the city was flooded with illegal weapons. A report in the *Independent* hit the linguistic nail on the head: 'The once-unfashionable Brummie accent could be a global money-spinner for the BBC'. The writer, Steven Knight, drew attention to the way the accent was typically portrayed on the screen:

> For some reason people slow the accent down and make it a really slow drawl. People have a peculiar relationship with the Birmingham accent because it's never done right on the telly, but if you hear people talking it's quite a hard, fast, urban accent. It's very intelligible; even an American will be able to understand it.

What I found most interesting was the way virtually every review I read started off with the accents – usually praising the intention, and then panning the result.

> It's actually refreshing to see Birmingham and its oft-mocked accent given a dramatic makeover. (*Metro*)

> Guns, gangs, anarchy and dodgy accents in post-World War One Birmingham. (*The Arts Desk*)

James Delingpole in the *Spectator* really laid into it:

> Let's start with the accents. Some sound like a mélange of Liverpool and generic northern; others sound Irish, even when spoken by characters who aren't supposed to be Irish. The series is set in Small Heath in 1919. Times have changed a bit since then, I'm sure, but Brummagem accents? I doubt it. Birmingham, by then, had had a good three centuries as one of the nation's industrial epicentres to establish its particular style and voice. More likely in this series they either a) couldn't be arsed, times being sloppy and voice coaching not being what it was, or b) deliberately chose not to make them real on account of the Brummie accent emerging in numerous polls as Britain's least popular, or c) they were worried it might jeopardise its chances with the US market.

And as the stories came out, it emerged that there had indeed been quite a bit of worry. The *Birmingham Post* reported Helen McCrory looking to a Birmingham-born actress for guidance about her accent:

> I got Julie Walters to sit down and do three pages of the *Peaky Blinders* script for me in a Brummie accent, which I recorded. I copied that but when I turned up to film, they said 'Oh no, we can't have that'. It was too thick. I was pretty much incomprehensible. We had a voice coach who said 'this is going to be the *Peaky Blinders* accent'.

So it's an artistically driven accent after all.

The series was hugely successful, but ironically it will have done little to remove the earlier stereotypes. The accent of the *Peaky Blinders* characters may have been more realistic, but as a result it didn't sound much like the Brummie stereotype at all, and reviewers didn't know what to make of it. It didn't fit the Brummie they remembered. Maybe, with further series being planned, a new status for the accent will emerge, but it will take more than one series to turn the linguistic fortunes of Birmingham around.

THE ROUGH AND THE SMOOTH

BEN   In 2004, I was given the most regular job I've ever had. Thirteen weeks of being the narrator to a *Big-Brother-*style TV series, set in a hairdressing and beauty salon. I learnt a lot about haircuts and shampoo over those spring months . . .

The series was being made in a converted printing factory in south London, full of dust, with video-editing rooms crammed into every corner. I had a recording booth which had no windows, and was barely soundproof, but it sufficed.

After a few weeks, the producers and I both came to a realization: it might be beneficial to all parties concerned if I left. They thought they might fire me for not making more people watch their show, while I was finding my throat aching at the end of each long day as I strained to give them what they wanted.

The problem was this: in order to keep the show running, and the ratings up, it was decided that the show needed to become sleazier; the direction from the young producers had begun to push the narratorial tone (that we'd spent so much time nailing down) to sound even rougher.

While waiting for the show to be edited together from whatever had transpired during the day's filming, they had insisted I watch previous episodes, to remind myself of my original narrator's voice, as if I had started speaking in grand RP without realizing it.

Now, I don't sound particularly public school, but I equally don't sound like I belong on *EastEnders* either. The number of times I'd been hired for a voice-over, and after the *click*, I'd heard,

Exec – It's great, but can you be a bit . . . rougher?

WHY DIDN'T YOU HIRE SOMEONE ROUGHER? I would silently scream, despite knowing that this is an odd thing to say, as all actors ever want is a role that pushes them from their natural self.

Rougher. If I had a penny . . . I'm quite happy not naturally sounding 'rough'. Rough is the thug, the big muscly fellow who usually dies a painful death at the end of a movie. The master-criminal part has the careful, well-spoken accent.*

I hear accents around me all the time, but I never think, Oh, that sounds 'rough', or That sounds 'refined'. Instead, Where are they from? is the question that jumps to my mind. Can I pin them down, James-Bond-style, to a particular corner of the world?

So, I was no longer the right voice-over artist for a TV show that had shed its skin and was becoming a monster: the producer's office had become a home for the casting book

---

* Admittedly, they usually die too, but at least there's a bit more glamour involved.

Freaks and Uniques 2004 as they scoured the land for more and more extreme folk to appear on their rapidly dying show.

I found myself spending long hours trying to bring lurid excitement into my voice at the prospect of someone deliberating over a back, sack and crack wax. My voice became deeper, my accent coarser and less articulate. 'Graphic and lewd' on screen demanded a lower, gravelly vocal register, and no consonants.

I couldn't give two figs for the show. I wanted to be an actor, and not just any actor, a *Shakespearean actor*. And: the new director of the National Theatre had promised me an audition for his opening Shakespeare production of *Henry V*, casting one of the best black Shakespearean performers in the UK as the lead.

Sometimes you'll get a fair amount of prep time before an audition. If you're lucky, you might find out two days beforehand, but even less time than that is the norm. My acting agent rang me with news that the National Theatre wanted to see me. An audition I could only have dreamed of. But they wanted to see me the next day, when I was supposed to be recording yet more voice-overs about hair.

Cut to that next day, sitting in the foyer of the National Theatre, after the audition. My phone rings. Jane, my voice agent:

J – WHAT THE HELL DID YOU SAY TO THEM? [Not shouting, but speaking in capitals as she often does when narked.]

– Um, what?

J – YOU'D BETTER DO SOME APOLOGIZING AND QUICK SHARP, MY LAD.

— Yes, Jane.

When the call for the audition had come in, the latest they could see me was at 5 p.m. The TV show went 'live' at 5.45 p.m. and often the second half of the episode was still being edited while the first half was playing out live to millions of viewers. In order to get to the audition in time, I needed to leave my recording booth by 4 p.m. at the latest.

The thing was, they always liked to keep me there until the episode was actually airing in case anything needed changing at the last moment. This particularly frantic, mad moment of panic happened around three or four times a week. It was kinda fun, the last-minute dash to word-perfectly record something that ten minutes later was being beamed to millions of viewers. But today was different.

– I have to leave early, I told the young producers.

They squirmed as if I was asking them to birth an ostrich, but finally said I was allowed to leave early. The exact second we finished recording the script – at a miraculously early 4.10 p.m. – I bolted out of the booth.

I was LEAVING. I was OUT OF THERE. I was only half-way across the studio floor when the Executive Producer, who did not seem particularly full of the joys of spring, snagged me.

EP – Where the hell are you going?

– I told them [the young producers], I have to go. It's important.

EP – I don't care what it is, you have to be here, he said, not unkindly. You can't just *go*.

And then I said, and I believe my exact words were,

– So, fire me then.

Yes, that's what I said. In the production office. In front of all the young producers. I challenged the Executive Producer to fire me.

It wasn't, it has to be said, my finest professional hour.

Thinking back, probably part of the reason he didn't is because I didn't say it arrogantly. I do seem to remember I said it casually, as the conversation ended, over my shoulder, like I didn't care, because I didn't care, because I was only thinking about whether or not I'd get the part. That or he couldn't find the book he wanted to throw at me.

But I was gone, off down a Shakespearean yellow-brick road.

Forty-five minutes later, I was staring at the floor. I had read what I'd prepared, and the director had just asked if I wouldn't mind making the character a bit more Cockney. I stared at the floor for a bit longer, and then did what, to a passer-by, probably sounded like a very bad Dick van Dyke impression, my nerves making me lose any sense of realism or truth to the reading.

I got a call from my acting agent the next day on the way to the hairdressing voice-over gig.

Agent – Hi, love. Yeah, National Theatre LOVED you. But they've decided to go with someone *rougher* . . .

When I got to the location for the TV show, I walked a slow ten thousand miles through the production office, sheepishly bearing a very expensive bottle of malt whisky for the EP. It was a very, very fine bottle of malt.

EP – Oh, no, this is too much, he said, as if he'd already fired me and so couldn't accept so costly a gift.

– Yesterday was important to me, but I shouldn't have spoken to you that way.

EP – We're all one family here; we could have helped if you'd have said.

Bullshit.

– Yes, I know.

I started to skulk off.

EP – Oh, and Ben?

– Yes? I turned, hopeful and smiling.

EP – Rougher today, OK? Yesterday wasn't rough enough. Get it?

– . . . OK. Rougher. Yep. Got it.

And I thereby managed to secure myself ten more weeks as a sleazy salonista. I went back to my booth to curl up and dye.

Flash forward to a competition on a London radio station in 2013. The local listener calling had to answer five questions in twenty seconds, and was told all the answers would begin with the same letter: F.

The first questions went by fine. The fourth though, hit a snag. The DJ cleared his throat.

DJ – OK, the fourth question: what's thirteen minus nine?

Listener – Free.

There was one of those radio silences that isn't supposed

to happen. Then a noise like a gasp, as if the DJ had been nudged in the ribs, waking him from a stupor. He cleared his throat again.

DJ – Well, no, it's four, but also, and I don't know how to tell you this . . .

Then, in early 2014, I overheard the following exchange in a clothes store in south London:

Friend 1 – Does it fit?

Friend 2 – Nah, it's too small. I'm gonna have to try a bigger size or summin'.

Friend 1 – Don't say it like that! You don't say 'summin''; you say 'someFINK'.

You may well be aware of this phenomenon: that there's a tendency in inner-city London accents to pronounce the *th* of *something* or *three* with an *f*. And over time, the *ng* of *something* has become a *k*. The consonants *g* and *k* are sounded with the same parts of the mouth and tongue: one engages the vocal cords and so is technically called 'voiced', *g*, and the other doesn't engage the vocal cords, so is described as 'voiceless', *k*.

Gently put your fingers against your throat, and say *guh* and then *kuh*, and you'll see what I mean.

The fact that the radio listener said *three* rather than *four* doesn't mean she's unintelligent. It's more likely she was nervous talking live on air. The fact that she said *free* rather than *three* doesn't mean she's ill-educated, either. It's a non-standard pronunciation of the word, just as *summin'* and *somefink* are non-standard soundings of the word *something*, and that sounding narrows down where the speakers grew up to a particular part of the country. No more, no less.

Now flash back to my teens, before I even knew what a London accent was. My first memory of noticing an accent in print was in school, and the character Donald Farfrae in Thomas Hardy's *The Mayor of Casterbridge*:

> My name is Donald Farfrae. It is true I am in the corren trade—but I have replied to no advertisement, and arranged to see no one. I am on my way to Bristol—from there to the other side of the warrld, to try my fortune in the great wheat-growing districts of the West! I have some inventions useful to the trade, and there is no scope for developing them heere.

I remember noticing the slightly odd spelling, and needing to ask my teacher, Mrs Black, whether it was meant to be a satire or an accurate copy of the Scots sound in the late nineteenth century.

But what came across most strongly to my teenage self, something I hadn't thought of much before, was the way the other characters instantly latched on to Farfrae's mode of dress and accent, the fact that he was, to them, different, alien – 'seemingly a Scotchman'. At that moment, there was electricity in the writing for me; even in a genteel Victorian novel, accents seemed to *matter*.

As I type, sitting across from me Dad is currently reading—

D – Scanning, dear boy.

. . . sorry, scanning, one hundred years' worth of the collated *Punch* annuals, classic satire from the nineteenth century that he bought last year. Let me clarify the image I am looking at: he has one very large stack of annuals on his right side, and a much smaller stack on his left. He's going through every page of slightly yellowed, tiny, antiquated print sketches and pieces, scouring them *all*, looking for articles, cartoons and jokes about language, Shakespeare . . . and of course, now, accents.* Every now and again he calls me over, I put down my quill, and amble over to see page after page of accent jokery. The way that we judge other accents is clearly not a new thing.†

And consider this, from Jen Campbell's 2012 book, *Weird Things Customers Say in Bookshops*:

> Bookseller: Would you like a bag? We've got plastic and paper ones.
>
> Customer: Well I would have asked for a bag, but you said 'plastic bag' not 'pla[r]stic bag', so now that you've said that I don't want one.
>
> Bookseller: I'm not sure people say 'pla[r]stic bag'. Also, I'm from Newcastle so I say 'bath' not 'ba[r]th'.
>
> Customer: Clearly you're uneducated.

---

* Seriously, you should try living with him.

† As it happens, the *Punch* pieces were quite interesting. The objects of satire were not quite the same as they are now. The Cockney and Scots accents are mocked mercilessly – but there's no mention of Brummie at all. As we saw in Dad's piece earlier, 'Brumagem' was an upmarket place back then, the beating heart of British industry, and certainly not somewhere to be caricatured.

This, as they say, actually happened. This, says Poppa C, is a dominant mindset of much of the twenty-first-century Western world: that we consider accent as indicative of educational background. If you have one accent, or speak one way, then you're thick. If you have another, you're immediately bestowed with qualities of culture, refinement, honesty, and integrity. Take Dick van Dyke in *Mary Poppins* (1964). The man sings and clowns like a minor god, but he sounds like a Londoner who got drunk on tequila for the first time and woke up in the Deep South. Whatever the quality of van Dyke's Cockney accent, we still understand what's happening: Dick's character, Bert, is amiable, innocent, naive – and working class.

Contrast this with the other end of the social scale. If you were a Hollywood actor a few years before *Poppins*, in the 1950s, and you wanted to perform Shakespeare, you had to sound like Laurence Olivier (and even he was considered lazy compared to the previous Shakespearean actor of the time, John Gielgud).* In the fifties, to be well dressed, well educated, and to speak well were the only things people cared about. You could – and people did – go around randomly slaying innocents and get away with it, as long as you didn't *sound* like a criminal.

Dad tells me that the beautiful RP accent of Olivier and Gielgud is actually only currently spoken by 2 per cent of the

---

* As we'll see later, the accent in Shakespeare's time actually sounds like a cross between *Pirates of the Caribbean* and English Country Yokel Who Has Spent Some Time In Ireland.

population of Britain, and yet it's still seen around the world as the quintessential British sound, despite Britain acoustically being made up of countless Scots, Irish, Welsh, regional English and international accents.

At some point in time, there must have been a switch in Hollywood, because for the last few decades if an English character was in an American movie then there were four options: they were either evil, posh, Cockney, or a pirate.

Or a combination of all four.

Somerset, or the West Country, is the part of England that has the accent we'd most associate with the ha-HARRRR of the stereotypical pirate voice.* It probably came from the fact that those are seafaring parts of the warrrld, the launching-off point from which Britain dominated the seven seas. Only a few miles away, in neighbouring Dorset, you'd find the gentle melody which formed the basis for the accent of the Shire and the Hobbits.

Regional British accents struggle in Hollywood,† and the strong, fast Glaswegian accent was comically subtitled in *Trainspotting* (1996), the film that made Ewan McGregor, a Scotsman whose native accent we rarely hear in his movies any more. But McGregor switched to RP when he made the three *Star Wars* prequels, as did his Sussex-born predecessor

---

* Incidentally, it's worth remembering that Johnny Depp's accent in the *Pirates* . . . movies is more East Anglia, towards Estuary English, despite being based on Rolling Stone Keith Richards, who was born in Kent. Both East Anglia and Kent lie the entire breadth of England away from the Somerset home of the 'Pirate' accent.

† See Don Cheadle, *Ocean's Eleven* (2001).

Sir Alec Guinness, to play Obi-Wan Kenobi – the only character in the series that used RP and wasn't Evil.

In fact, as I think about it, all of the villains in *Star Wars*
have an RP accent – except Darth Vader, who was played by
David Prowse but whose voice was later edited out and re-
recorded with the rich basso-profundo tones of American
actor James Earl Jones.

Jaguar's Superbowl 2014 commercial featured Ben Kingsley, Tom Hiddleston and Mark Strong, all British actors
currently well known for their portrayal of super-villains. In
the ad, the actors discuss this point, and explain that 'we're
more focused', and maybe 'we just sound right'.

A 'stiff-upper lip is key' continues the ad, and perhaps that
is indeed the key to sounding Evil: that not allowing your
emotions to make your lip wobble, and keeping a controlled,
clear articulation are at the heart of the accent of the upper
classes and their establishing rule. To lead by example, and
be emotionless in the face of opposition – while still sounding
utterly *charming* – are fairly go-to qualities in a megaloma-
niac, power-obsessed villainous cad.

The ad points out that Brits are 'obsessed by power', and
it's true that from Captain Hook in *Peter Pan* (1953) and *Hook*
(1991), to Jeremy Irons's Scar in *Lion King* (1994) or Alan
Rickman in *Die Hard* (1988), RP has been used to radiate the
idea of power. I suppose there are two corollaries of this: a
Brit is somehow safer to portray as evil, in terms of the
message a film is wanting to make, than say a Middle-Eastern
actor. And it handily taps in to the inherent image that still

lingers in many minds, of a conquering people whose Empire never knew a sunset.

Let's not forget there are just twenty-two countries in the world out of 196 or so that Britain *hasn't* invaded (including the Vatican City, Luxembourg and Sweden). Now, of course I'm not suggesting that producers in Hollywood have a big map on their office wall, and think, Hm, Holland hasn't invaded anyone for a while, so we can't have a Dutch bad guy; where's England up to?

But it can't be a coincidence that so many – Terence Stamp in *Superman* (1978), Ben Kingsley in *Iron Man 3* (2013), Snake in *The Simpsons* (1989–), Ian McKellen in *X-Men* (2000), most of the bad guys in the James Bond films, and all but one in *Star Wars*, to name but a few – all speak in the same posh English accent. Can it, Dad?

WHY DO THE BAD GUYS TALK POSH?

DAVID   To explain what's going on, the first thing we have to do is be clear about what 'talking posh' means. As Ben's said, it refers to the originally upper-class accent in England that for the last hundred years or so has been called RP. When people talk about it, they usually think of the speech of the Queen, or the traditional sound of the BBC, or the voices emanating from institutions such as Oxford and Cambridge universities, the leading public schools, or the Church of England. In a desperate attempt to capture its character, it's been called a 'cut-glass' accent – a term that reflects its fashionable origins among the aristocracy. Linguists describe it more neutrally: it's a social accent that conveys no infor-mation at all about where in England you come from. If you speak RP, you don't show your geographical origins. You do, however, show your social origins, or how you were educated. And you will almost certainly be a member of the country's professional elite.

We would, then, expect the characters played by British movie professionals to talk posh, whether they're good guys or bad. Those played by Laurence Olivier, John Gielgud,

Ralph Richardson, and others in the mid-twentieth century illustrate that trend: whether from Hamlet or Richard III, it was RP that moviegoers heard. But fast-forward into the later decades of the century and things are not so simple. Even the good guys don't always talk posh. Take James Bond.

We'd expect Bond to speak RP – but what we get (in the first five Bond films) is a Scottish-modulated Sean Connery. I focus on him because Bond's biographers tell us that Connery's portrayal influenced Ian Fleming's development of the character. In *You Only Live Twice*, we learn that he was the son of a Scottish father, Andrew Bond, and a Swiss mother, Monique Delacroix. The young James lived abroad a lot because of his father's work. But his parents were killed when he was eleven, and he completed his education in England, briefly attending Eton College and later Fettes College in Edinburgh. An educated Scots accent is what we'd expect to hear as a result, and that is what we get in Connery, who was born in Edinburgh.

His accent is not only not-RP, it is highly individual. It's a voice that is easily recognizable, thanks to certain distinctive features – notably, his pronunciation of *s* and *z*, where his tongue is often further back in the mouth than normal, and curling towards the hard palate, resulting in a sound more like 'sh'. Technically, it's called a 'retroflex s', and it's quite common in Scotland and Ireland (Connery had an Irish father), though it may in his case be an idiosyncratic lisp-like feature. His accent is an interesting blend of working-class and middle-class Scots sounds, as well as having echoes of the kind of English he would most often have encountered in the film industry. It certainly isn't a broad Scots accent – no strongly trilled *r*, for example – but it's not an English accent either. It's definitely local to the part of Scotland where he grew up – which is what I'd expect, given Connery's strong views about accents and identity: 'I am not an Englishman, I was never an Englishman, and I don't ever want to be one. I am a Scotsman!' . . . 'To cultivate an English accent is already a step and a departure away from what you are.'

He would therefore be horrified to hear his voice described as 'English' in the American press. But such things are normal. It's very difficult for people to hear accent differences from a country other than their own, and they blithely call everything 'British' or 'American' or 'Australian'. British people don't hear the differences between the various American accents – or, if they do hear them, they aren't able to identify them, and they certainly don't have any sense of the social attitudes associated with them. People outside of Britain have a similar inability when it comes to British accents – as we've seen in the case of Birmingham. Americans who are aware of Connery's Scots identity will of course readily call his accent 'Scottish' without really knowing what it is that makes it so. But they might just as readily call him, and it, 'British'. For most Americans, there's a 'British accent', and that's all that needs to be said. As RP is the version they've most often heard in the classic movies where a British actor has an important role, the equation is obvious. British accent = RP. And with RP comes the historical baggage of its social and cultural associations.

The origins of RP

RP is actually quite a recent accent, in the history of English. There was no RP in Shakespeare's day, as we'll see later. The accent evolved around the very end of the eighteenth century. That century was one in which elegant London society came to be acknowledged as the source of all good manners and fashion, and the pronunciation of its members played an important part in showing the new class distinctions in Britain, with an industrial middle-class elbowing its way in between the traditional opposition of upper and lower. The writer William Kenrick observed in the 1770s:

> By being properly pronounced, I would be always under-stood to mean, pronounced agreeable to the general practice of men of letters and polite speakers in the Metropolis.

And what was that general practice? To speak in a way that was as distant as possible from the way people spoke in the provinces or (even more to be avoided) in the East End of London.

So, if Cockneys dropped their *h*s, polite society would not. If Cockneys put an *h* in where it wasn't in the spelling (as in 'I broke my harm'), polite society would not. If people from the provinces pronounced an *r* after a vowel, polite society would not. Gradually, a new accent emerged, and John Walker – the author of the leading pronouncing dictionary of the age – used the term that would subsequently become its defining feature:

> though the pronunciation of London is certainly errone-
> ous in many words, yet, upon being compared with that
> of any other place, it is undoubtedly the best; that is, not
> only the best by courtesy, and because it happens to be
> the pronunciation of the capital, but the best by a better
> title – that of being more generally received.

Received from whom? From fashionable society, and in particular from the court and the aristocracy. During the nineteenth century, we see the accent routinely called the King's English or (under Victoria) the Queen's English.

By the end of the century, RP had become a technical term. The pioneering phonetician Alexander Ellis summed it up: we may, he said, 'recognize a received pronunciation all over the country', adding that 'it may be especially considered as the educated pronunciation of the metropolis, of the court, the pulpit and the bar', and he later added other categories, such as the universities and the stage. It was he who first abbreviated it as *r.p.* (The capitals came later.)

'All over the country . . .' Clearly, during the nineteenth century, RP travelled. Educated people from different parts of Britain increasingly came into contact with each other – thanks especially to the new railway network. More people were going to university than ever before. And we see the growth of the prestigious boarding-school system for boys. The Public Schools Act of 1868 gave the first legal definition to seven such schools, including Eton, Rugby, Winchester, and Westminster, and these formed a widespread community united as much by its attention to pronunciation as by its attention to dress and the well-off family background of its pupils.

The public-school system was such a powerful movement in fostering an upper-class accent that, when the great twentieth-century phonetician Daniel Jones (the model for George Bernard Shaw's Professor Henry Higgins in *Pygmalion*) made his first description of it, he actually called it 'Public School Pronunciation'. He renamed it RP in 1926, recalling Ellis's usage – by which time, it had also been adopted by the newly formed BBC. Lord Reith, the BBC's founder, was in no doubt that his organization needed 'uniformity of pronunciation' so that broadcasts would be understood by as many people as possible. He sought 'a common denominator of educated speech', and he found it in RP.

But RP didn't just travel around Britain. It went around the world. The products of the public-school system, after a period at Oxford or Cambridge, would become the core of the Anglican Church, whose missionaries abroad would give the accent an international reach. Above all, these schoolboys would grow up to become the backbone of the civil and diplomatic service, giving the British Empire its public voice, and making RP an accent 'on which the sun never sets'. By the time talking movies arrived, in the 1930s, RP was already firmly in place as the public voice of Britain on the world stage.

The American perspective

With the early dominance of Hollywood, most of the first talking-picture stars were American, and character actors – especially those playing villains – had to come from elsewhere. No actor who was famous – or who wanted to become famous – would dream of having a heroic or romantic image tarnished by playing a villain. And as cinema was primarily an English-language medium, the obvious place to look for villains who spoke the same language was Britain. That meant RP.

It's of interest to note that RP was developing in Britain at the same time as Britain and America were fighting the War of Independence. Language and identity being so closely linked, it's hardly surprising that attitudes related to the political outcome would be reflected in linguistic antagonisms. And in the period following the War of Independence, and the much less-remembered War of 1812, relations between Britain and America were at an all-time low. In such a climate, British accents would certainly be considered villainous by Americans (and vice versa, of course).

Tribal memories have a long shelf-life. Even though political relations between the two countries became fraternal during the nineteenth century, mutual criticism and condemnation of pronunciation is frequently recorded. And emotions were still high during the early decades of the twentieth, when broadcasting began nationally in the USA, and decisions had to be made about the kind of accent to use on air.

Lord Reith's decision to use RP was noted. But when some of the first radio announcers tried out an imitation-British accent, an American observer, Josiah Combs, condemned them outright as 'foolish and stupid'. In a 1931 article in the journal *American Speech* he described what he called the 'Oxford pronunciation' as 'the most offensive and illogical in the English-speaking world':

> It is merely a link in the chain of icy exclusiveness long practised and fostered by loyal Oxfordians and their representatives in politics and among the landlording classes. It does not hesitate to assimilate, slur, chop, swallow and cut; in short, it stoops to anything in pronunciation that will make it as difficult as possible for average folks to imitate.

Icy exclusiveness. Landlording. Villains!

The feeling was mutual. H. L. Mencken, reviewing the early history of pronunciation attitudes in his book *The American Language*, summarizes the typical early twentieth-century response of the British to American accents, and talks again of tribal memories. Their discomfort, he says, 'relights in them the old passionate conviction of their nation that everything American is not only inferior, but also villainous and ignoble. Thus their typical attitude to the gabble of Americans . . . is one of utter loathing'. Villainous again.

So, if you were directing a talkie in the 1930s, this is the kind of linguistic climate in which you would be working. It's hardly surprising, then, to find British voices being used for the bad guys, or indeed for any characters other than the romantic and heroic leads. And the impression has grown up that this was always the case. At a film event in Los Angeles in 2010, Helen Mirren complained about it: 'I think it's rather unfortunate that the villain in every movie is always British. We're such an easy target that they can comfortably make the Brits the villains.'

In every movie? A complete accent filmography would find that a bit of an overstatement. RP does, after all, sometimes come out of good guys. As Ben's mentioned, think of Alec Guinness in *Star Wars*, or the various roles played by Hugh Grant or Colin Firth, or Julie Andrews and Dick van Dyke in *Mary Poppins*. And accents other than RP do sometimes come out of bad guys – especially in the days following periods of war (including the Cold War). German, Russian, and East Asian accents were all used, as long as they weren't too broad.

On the other hand, there are many iconic performances which do support the association of RP with evil. They date from the earliest decades of talking cinema. A classic example is *The Adventures of Robin Hood* (1938). The hero: Errol Flynn. The bad Guy (de Gisborne): Basil Rathbone. And in the many remakes, Sheriffs of Nottingham would continue to be RP speakers. Thinking back over my favourite movies, I can add to Ben's list, recalling case after case where the villains speak RP. *North by Northwest* (1959). The good guy: Cary Grant, very American. The bad guy: James Mason, very RP. There's the RP of Robert Shaw as SPECTRE's assassin in *From Russia With Love* (1963) and George Sanders as Shere Khan in *The Jungle Book* (1967). In *Die Hard* (1988), we have the good cop played by Bruce Willis, and the mastermind played by Alan Rickman – German, but with an RP accent. And to show the trend continuing into the new century, we have Benedict Cumberbatch playing an RP-speaking genetically superhuman bad guy in *Star Trek Into Darkness* (2013).

Any reader will be able to add to this list. At the same time, it's important to keep the ears phonetically alert. Just because an evil character is British doesn't mean that he or she will necessarily speak in RP. Anthony Hopkins as Hannibal Lecter doesn't in *The Silence of the Lambs* (1991). Laurence Olivier in *Marathon Man* (1976) has a German-tinged accent. So does Michael Collins, who kept an element of German in his accent when his voice was used instead of the (non-English-speaking) Gert Fröbe in *Goldfinger* (1964). But the voices all have one thing in common: they don't sound American. And they do all retain traces of the actors' original British accents.

So, even without RP, the bad guys do on the whole remain evilly British – unless their accent really doesn't suit the character. Let's return to Ben's excellent example from the *Star Wars* trilogy. There's a fascinating clip on YouTube showing a rehearsal in which we see Darth Vader played by the physically imposing Dave Prowse. We hear his voice behind the mask – a soft British accent, suggestive of Prowse's West Country origins (he was born in Bristol). It was the first time the producers had heard him talk in character, and they didn't like it. We hear one of them asking, 'Is it going to be some Scottish guy? What IS this?' Clearly, they had no idea what accent it was. But they knew it wasn't right. They wanted a darker, more menacing voice, and in the end it was dubbed by the deep bass of Mississippi-born James Earl Jones.* In a case like this, vocal timbre turns out to be far more important than accent.

The theme of the good little guy standing up against the bad powerful guy and winning is a recurring theme of American movies. And because RP was the accent of the rich and powerful, it was a natural choice for the bad guy. If there had been a home-grown aristocratic accent in the USA, corresponding to RP in Britain, the film-makers would doubtless have used that; but there was no such thing. RP was the obvious alternative and, as Helen Mirren felt, the easy target. But times are changing. Regionally modified British accents are widespread these days, as illustrated by the London tones of popular actors like Michael Caine, Bob Hoskins, and Ray Winston. And RP itself has changed, as we'll show later. Whatever movie accents were like in the twentieth century, they'll be very different in the twenty-first.

---

* B – Clearly enunciated Good American is more evil than, *Yurr ability t'destroy t'planeht is insignificahn next t'powuh of t'farce.*

PART TWO

ACCENTS PRESENT

MAPPING ACCENTS

BEN AND DAVID

– Hello.

– Hello.

– Dad, I need you to draw me a map.

– Yes, of what?

– An accent map. Of the British Isles.

– Ah, can't be done.

– What?

– It's impossible.

– No, it isn't, Dad.

– It is; it's impossible.

– No it isn't, Dad. I've just seen a bunch on Google Images.

– They won't be accurate. It can't be done well. I can show you. It's too complex. It's imposs—

– Stop saying it's impossible, nothing's impossible, some things are very, very difficult, but—

– Can't be d—

– Look: Cockney! Scouse! Geordie! It's not rocket science, it's easy, and while I could send a Google image to the book's illustrator, I want to send one that's accurate, and I know it'll be that if you've done it.

Dad, having turned away the last thirty seconds, comes back with a book.

– Y'see, the thing is, Geordie is located in a city, so is Scouse in Liverpool, and Cockney in London. They're easy. But accents like Somerset are heard in areas that don't always coincide with a county. How are we going to show that?

– How would I know? I'm not an illustrator. Maybe we capitalize the city-bound accents and don't capitalize the areas? Like the regions the Thanes ruled over in Macbeth's time, the borders of each Thane's land is vague, we can have broad swathes.

– But accents can change from town to town in England. It's like the last bit of the weather report when they show you Edinburgh–Belfast–London–Cardiff, and you think, Well, if I'm in Wrexham or Worcester I'm fine because I'm covered by bleeding Cardiff.

– Argh! You're looking too precisely on the point. We just need to cover the accents we talk about in this book. Americans might be familiar with the location of Wales, but how many know where the Geordie accent is, or how close it is in relation to Yorkshire, or Scouse to Mancunian?

– Hm, true. And a lot of Brits couldn't tell you where Virginia is.

– Right? I don't think I could point to it on a map.

– Hm.

– What?

– . . .

– I'm ignoring that 'Hm'. So, good. Now, what about South Africa?

– What about South Africa?

– I mean I don't know where an Afrikaans accent is spoken; do we need a map for that?

– Ah, well, South Africa is—

– Do not say, 'It's complicated.'

– Tricky, I was about to say.

– Well, do they all sound like [insert stereotypically nasal South African accent].

– Ah, no; that's the Afrikaans-influenced accent. The blacks don't. In fact many whites don't either. You have to think about it like being the difference between Crocodile Dundee and most Australians.

– OK . . .

– Do you know the difference?

– Yes.*

– You can find RP in Australia you know.

– WHAT?

– People think there's no accent differences in Oz—

– Hm, even I perceived the differ—

– But there didn't use to be, you see. We've only had two hundred years of English in Oz. Accents have developed, but much slower than in Britain because of the way Australia was colonized. There was a single point of entry – Australia was developed by colonizers moving out from Sydney in all directions. No one started out from Perth. Over here, the Anglo-Saxons arrived from different parts of northern Europe, and then settled in different parts of England, and so

---

* Lie.

their accents mutated into different animals. This didn't happen in Australia. Or in Canada. So a single accent spoken by military governors, soldiers, politicians – the ruling classes, essentially, all of whom would have spoken RP, spreads over the country.

– Dad, you sound like a linguistic Sherlock Holmes.

– Hm. Is that good?

– Yes.

– Cool.

– Saying 'cool' isn't, though, I'm afraid.

– Oh. What do people say now?

– I think it's 'metal'.

– Oh. I'm not saying that.

– Good. Now, about this map—

– Anyway, the convicts sent to Australia arrived from London, Liverpool, Northern Ireland and all over the place. Their accents melted together and provided a basis for class distinction via accent right from the beginning.

– So those accents became a new Australian mix of all our lower-class accents?

– Yes, and so, to an Australian, the accent Paul Whatsis-name uses in the *Crocodile Dundee* film is basically what the original 'convict accent' now sounds like, and is markedly different from – Hang on, why are you writing all this down?

– You'll see.

– But this will get complicated. We have to make sure our narrative voices are clear. *You* can't start talking about the history of accents. It won't sound right.

– Dad—

– I haven't started talking about the history of theatre—

– Dad, you'll see, I'm going to write a chapter about me coming into your study and suggesting a map, and the dialogue that unfurled, and the questions I asked you, because these are the questions I think people want to know the answers to. And that way, we can lay out in detail what the accents of English ARE, before we go deeper into what they once were, and where they might be going.

– Ah . . .

– . . . So it'll stay in your voice . . . Y'see?

– Hm.

The eyebrows unfurled.

– That's very good.

– Ta. And then in the next part of the book, we can write about how those distinct British city accents fused together.

– Hm. I'm not— No, what do you mean?

– Well, y'know, so Burglar Bill arrives in Sydney speaking Cockney, but his grandson speaks 'convict-Australian', and *his* grandson . . . What's happening? Then we finish the book talking about the future of accents. Maybe the death of accents? *Do* accents die? That sort of thing.

– I hate collaboration.

– I know you do. I'm only glad it's me that has to put up with you rather than some poor other—

– What was that?

– Nothing, Dad.

The 'Impossible' Map: Place-names and accent-names of the British Isles

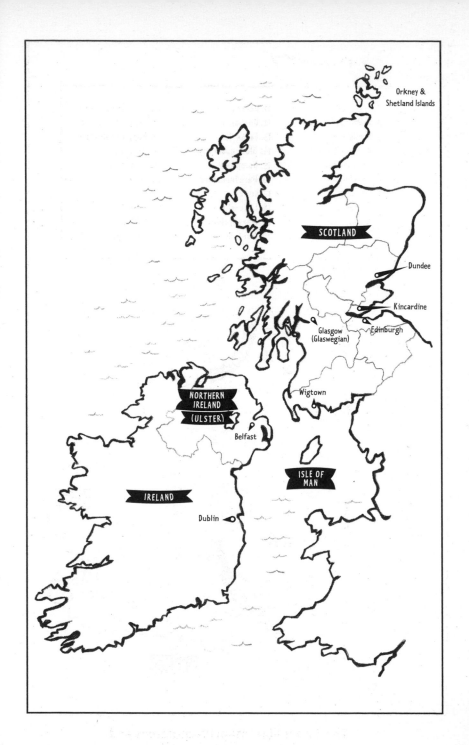

Orkney &
Shetland Islands

SCOTLAND

Dundee

Kincardine

Glasgow
(Glaswegian)

Edinburgh

NORTHERN
IRELAND
(ULSTER)

Wigtown

Belfast

ISLE OF
MAN

IRELAND

Dublin

See p. 86

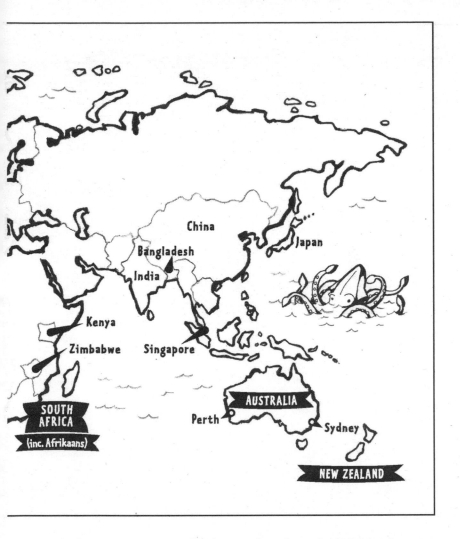

The countries we talk about other than the British Isles

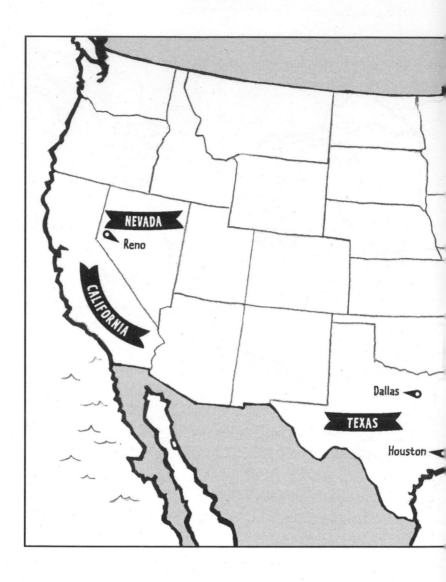

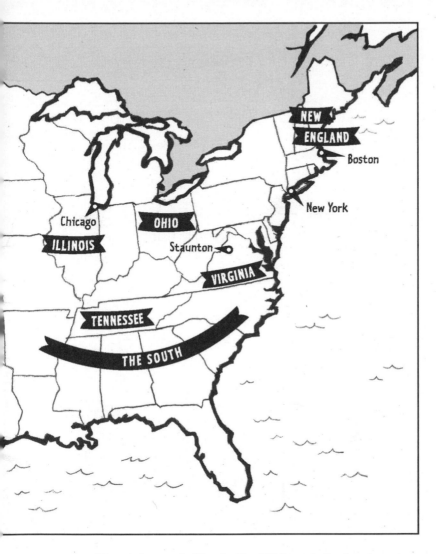

The states and cities in the USA we talk about

ACCENT DETECTIVES

DAVID [AND BEN]   They're around today, but it takes a lot of training and fieldwork to become really accomplished. Stanley Ellis was one. He worked on the Survey of English Dialects during the 1960s, and spent a decade travelling all over England, living out of a caravan, to tape-record interviews with local people. He later became well known on BBC Radio 4 for his series *Talk of the Town, Talk of the Country*. Less well known – until a momentous event took place – was his work as an expert witness in court cases where voice recordings were part of the evidence of speaker identification. This is forensic phonetics.

[B – DUMMM-duh-duh-dum]

Forensic phoneticians are busy people. Cases requiring voice analysis turn up quite often, and they are very time-consuming because of the amount of listening involved. A typical case would be an anonymous threat made over the phone. The phone call has been recorded. A suspect is named and interviewed, and that too is recorded. The job of the forensic phonetician is then to determine whether the voices on the two recordings are the same.

The evidence will come from the voice quality of the speakers, idiosyncratic vocal mannerisms, and of course their accents. I recall being asked to advise on such a case once, and although the tape recordings were only a minute or so, it took many hours of repeated listening to be sure I'd identified all of the distinctive features, and then further hours writing up a report in terms that phonetically untrained policemen and lawyers would be able to understand. But it was certainly possible to arrive at a recommendation. Sometimes the conclusions are positive: I am 90 per cent certain that two voices are the same. Sometimes they're negative: I am 80 per cent certain that two voices are different. It's rare indeed for the evidence to be so clear that there is 100 per cent certainty, one way or the other.

The momentous event that brought Stanley Ellis and other phoneticians into the limelight was the case of the Yorkshire Ripper, Peter Sutcliffe, who was eventually convicted of killing thirteen women between 1975 and 1980. By mid-1979, the police had made little progress. Then a series of handwritten letters arrived, claiming to be from the killer, followed in June by an audio cassette. 'I'm Jack,' the tape began, 'I see you are still having no luck catching me.' It went on for three minutes and sixteen seconds.

The detective in charge of the case was convinced the tape was genuine, and valuable time and resources were devoted to following it up. He set up Dial-the-Ripper phone lines. The public could ring in and listen to the voice, in the hope that someone would recognize it. The police turned to phoneticians to establish where the tape voice came from. Stanley

Ellis was one. Jack Windsor Lewis, also at the University of Leeds, was another. The Ripper tape had 257 words in it, and the recording was good. It was fairly obvious that the speaker came from the north-east of England. The media had already dubbed him 'Wearside Jack'. But which part, exactly? The phoneticians identified the voice as coming from Sunderland, and then visited the pubs and clubs of the town to narrow it down. They concluded that the voice was of someone who had been brought up in the Castletown or Southwick districts, near the river.

Was the tape genuine? The Sunderland accent is one of the most difficult to mimic, if you're not from the area. There was no indication that the voice on the tape was disguised. Unless you're a brilliant impressionist – or an expert phonetician – disguised voices tend to be rather inconsistent. Even then, they're not usually accurate. Impressionists tend to exaggerate certain features in order to make an effect. The tape voice wasn't like that. Moreover, there were certain idiosyncratic features of articulation. One word had an unusual quality for the sound *l*, and the word *sorry* had a lengthened *s*.

The voice was certainly distinctive, and the phoneticians were sure it would be quickly recognized. If this man had been living in Yorkshire, where the murders took place, his voice would have stood out a mile. The man had to be living on Wearside, where the voice would not have been so identifiable. They were sure it was a hoax. They wrote to the police, but their warning went unheeded. Suspects continued to be eliminated from enquiries if they had no Wearside accent.

Angry that their warnings had been disregarded, Jack Windsor Lewis went public in the *Yorkshire Post* on 3 December 1980. But it proved unnecessary to take the consequences of his article into account. Sutcliffe was caught a month later. He was from Bradford.

After years of speculation about his identity, the hoaxer was finally caught through DNA evidence in 2005, and pleaded guilty at a trial a few months later. He had been living in Flodden Road, just south of the river, less than a mile from Castletown. And he had gone to school in Castletown. The phoneticians had been right in their analysis. Henry Higgins would have been proud of them.

[B – Hang on, Dad, let's have a little backstory here. You mentioned earlier that George Bernard Shaw created the character Professor Henry Higgins for his play *Pygmalion* – but Higgins is probably more widely known in that play's adaptation, *My Fair Lady*, where he identifies himself as a practitioner of phonetics:

> The science of speech. That's my profession, also my hobby. Anyone can spot an Irishman or a Yorkshireman by his brogue, but I can place a man within six miles. I can place him within two miles in London. Sometimes within two streets.

OK, backstory over, my question is: could he actually have done this?]

Henry Higgins may be a fictitious character, but I mentioned earlier that he was based on a real-life professor of phonetics, Daniel Jones of University College London.

Shaw was hugely impressed by Jones's phonetics laboratory, and visited it several times. He carefully noted the newly developed methods of phonetic transcription for accurately writing down the sounds of speech – as we see Higgins doing when he first hears Eliza Dolittle on a London street. And he must have been struck by the ability of Jones and his colleagues to identify and reproduce English accents – and not just those of the present day. Jones sometimes did party pieces where he reproduced an original Shakespearean accent to the delight of the guests.

As Higgins says, anyone can place accents in a very general way. Most people can identify the main accent distinctions in a country – in Britain, the chief Celtic accents (Wales, Scotland, Ireland) or those from large areas such as 'West Country' or 'the North' or the accents of the major cities, such as Newcastle, Liverpool and Birmingham. And most people will have a go at 'doing' accents, even though what comes out is often a bit of a pastiche – a pirate 'oo-ar' for the West Country, for instance. It can be great fun – as the new (2014) parlour game, Accentuate, illustrates.

Ability tends to lessen as the locations become more specific. If you're not from the area, it's not so easy to tell the differences between, say, Lancashire and Yorkshire, or Cornwall and Devon, or Glasgow and Edinburgh. If you are, of course, then your ability would be much greater. When I was wandering around Wales for the BBC in 2005, making a television programme about English accents, I repeatedly met people from one town who would say they could tell someone from another town just a short distance away – 'within six miles', as it were – and proved it by giving me examples of different pronunciations. Such tiny differences do exist, therefore – there's an accent shift, on average, every twenty-five miles in England – so it's perfectly possible, in principle, for an expert to spend a lifetime studying them and becoming adept at identifying them. And some phoneticians I know are able to do just that.

The most famous was undoubtedly Henry Lee Smith, a twenty-seven-year-old professor of English at Brown University, Rhode Island, who in 1940 began to present a radio series called *Where Are You From?*. It went out at 8 p.m. each Wednesday from the Mutual Broadcasting Company playhouse at New York City's New Amsterdam Roof (a former nightclub, located above the home of the Ziegfeld Follies). Each week, a group of people whom Smith had never met before were selected from the audience. The contestants were given a set of twenty words to pronounce, such as *very*, *any*, *wash*, *greasy*, and *on*, and including word sets such as *marry*, *merry*, and *Mary*; and on the basis of their responses Smith would tell them where they were from. If he was exactly right, a peal of five tubular bells would be rung in celebration. If he was almost right, four. It was rare for fewer than three bells to be heard. Smith was correct seven out of ten times, even sometimes homing in on specific neighbourhoods in a big city (such as Brooklyn, Manhattan, or the Bronx in New York).

An article in the magazine *Radio Parade* called Smith's ability 'uncanny', and labelled him a 'voice detective'. In fact – as Smith himself said – any well-trained phonetician who has specialized in English accents would be able to do what he did, though how many of them would have Smith's panache, charisma, and ability to perform in the public eye is another matter. It was certainly a virtuoso linguistic perform-ance. And the amazing thing, to my mind, is that he was doing this in the USA – a country which is over forty times the size of Britain. It's one thing to pinpoint someone coming from the middle of Cornwall; a much more ambitious task to place them in the middle of California.

Where Are You From? was a hugely successful series, continuing for several years, with later broadcasts being filmed and transmitted by Kinescope on local television stations. Judging by the pictures in the March 1941 edition of the magazine *Radio Parade*, it was great fun. Celebrities came on the show to add interest. There was an amateur accent sleuth, Tom Horon, who had a slot where he pitted his skills against Smith. And each week there was a mystery guest, allowing the audience to have a go themselves. The guest would read a little jingle:

> Said Mercenary Mary
> The man that I would marry
> Must be merry and adroit about the house
> He must not take it easy
> While the dinner pots are greasy
> The simple cheerful man that I'd espouse.

The best five guesses would be awarded money prizes. At the end of the show, there was a rapid-fire sequence involving five members of the audience, in which Smith had thirty seconds to talk to each one and work out where they were from. He was usually right.

[B – OK, so could it be done now? Can *you* do it, for that matter?]

Smith would have a much greater problem today because of accent mixture. He was at his most successful when faced with someone who had lived their whole life in a single place, and travelled little, and who thus had a 'pure' accent. If not, he faced problems. It's not so hard to distinguish the strands in a person whose accent is a mixture of two locations. But if their background reflects three or more, it's virtually impossible to disentangle them, as similar vowel qualities could be the result of many interactions.

[B – That's a 'no', then.]

Smith had real trouble with the character actor Dudley Digges, for example, whom he placed in Chillicothe, Ohio. In fact, Digges was an Irish immigrant who had lived in California, New York, and elsewhere, and had performed Hollywood roles in a variety of voices. No bells for Smith on that occasion – but no shame either. Actors are the worst people in the world to locate. Ben's current accent could – depending on who he's currently 'being' – reflect any place or time. As I write, it's hovering somewhere around London in 1600.

[B – 1602, to be precise.]

It wouldn't have been too hard for Professor Higgins to justify his 'six miles' claim in Britain at the end of the nineteenth century. A century ago, the mass of the population lived their whole lives – apart from the occasional holiday excursion – in one place. Their accent would thus have been 'pure' – internally consistent, and shared by others in their local community. It's very different a hundred years on, in a travelling, commuting, resettling age. According to a Bosch survey in 2013, the average UK resident will move house eight times during a lifetime – census data suggests that it's eleven times in the USA – and one in five end up living over 200 miles from where they started out. The moves include all kinds of accommodation, of course, such as childhood homes, university digs, flat shares, and first-time houses, but the important thing is not what one lives in, but how well people integrate within their new community.

It doesn't take long for an accent to shift once someone settles down. If you like your new neighbours, you'll start to talk like them – another example of the accommodation process we talked about earlier. (If you don't, of course, you're likely to stick with your original accent, and even exaggerate it, to show you're different.) A common experience is for people to pay a visit to where they formerly lived, and to hear relatives and friends say they sound different. My wife comes from Hertfordshire, and people in North Wales, where we now live, often comment on the southern accent in her voice. But when she goes back to Hertfordshire, she's more than once been told she sounds Welsh.

[B – Ha! You sound like a Scouse mongrel at the best of times.]

Do you mind! My own accent is a mix of the places I've lived in – Wales, Liverpool, London, Berkshire. That means it isn't an entirely consistent accent. Sometimes I say *example*, with a short *a*; sometimes *exahmple*. I never know which it's going to be; it depends a lot on the person I'm talking to. Generational differences are also going to be an influence, as we discussed in the Introduction with *shedule* and *skedule*.

Mixed accents are the norm these days. Even if you don't travel, you're not immune from accent shift. Innumerable voices enter your home every day through radio, television, the telephone, and the Internet. In 2013 a team of researchers from the University of Glasgow published the results of a study in the journal *Language* which showed that certain features of the typical Glasgow accent were changing among young people partly as a result of prolonged exposure to the London-based BBC TV soap *EastEnders*. They were increasingly replacing *th* by *f* (in words like *tooth* and *think*) and replacing *l* by a vowel (so that *milk*, for example, comes out more like 'miuk').

If any programme is going to affect accents, *EastEnders* will. Half-hour episodes go out four times a week, with repeats and an omnibus edition – over 4,700 episodes broadcast by 2014. That's a lot of listening. The programme has been watched by almost a third of the UK population, and attracts widespread discussion of characters and plot. The emotional engagement of the viewers is frequently attested by the way a social issue dealt with on the programme impacts on real life – for example, in 2006 a storyline about bipolar disorder won a Mental Health Media Award. With such an influence, it's very likely that the Cockney accents of the characters will begin to rub off onto viewers. Mockney, it's sometimes called. We'll talk more about this later.

This isn't the first time television has been identified as a factor in accent change. A high rising pitch on statements ('I'll see you at the párty?') became popular among British teenage girls during the 1980s. It crossed the gender divide, and rapidly spread up the age range, despite it often being criticized by older people. But it hasn't gone away. It provides a conveniently succinct way of 'checking' that one's listener is on the same wavelength. 'I'll see you at the pàrty', with a falling tone, is definite: we both know which party it is. 'I'll see you at the párty?', with a rising pitch, is less so: I know which party it is, and I'm checking that you do too. Where did this usage come from? The Australian television soap *Neighbours*.

'Come from' is a bit of an overstatement. What television actually does is not so much introduce a brand-new feature of accent, as reinforce a trend that may already be in the community, or take an existing feature and move it in a different direction. *EastEnders* wasn't the first time young Glaswegians would have heard those accent features, nor would *Neighbours* have been the first time youngsters heard a rising tone on statements. But these programmes do foster a talking community in which people playfully imitate what they have heard, and gradually assimilate some of the features into their everyday speech.

Quite often, when I meet someone for the first time, and when they learn I'm a linguist and discover what linguists do, they say smugly, 'I bet you can't tell where I'm from.' I never take the bet. Mixed accents mean that it's no longer so easy to identify where people come from, just by listening to their voices. But it can still be done, as the field of forensic phonetics—

[B – DUMMM-duh-duh-dum-DAAAAA]

. . . shows.

CASTING FOR ACCENTS

BEN   When I was training to be an actor, I was told that I might have a good voice for radio, but what seemed of equal importance to having good tones was that I was pretty proficient at accents. After graduating I paid to have a voice-over demo reel made: sixty seconds of vocal gymnastics in various brogues, bounded in 10–15-second fragments of manufactured radio commercials. The scripts had been specially written to sound like real radio or TV ads in order to demonstrate my range, though the products were all fictitious.

Having a natural modified RP accent (again, listen to the cut-glass accent of Laurence Olivier's Hamlet, but then think less manicured, a bit more gravelly, and generally, well, a bit *casual*, I suppose you could say), I could easily swing my voice to sound the accents I'd lived around: of Wales, Lancashire, and London. I could also take fairly good stabs at different parts of Ireland, Somerset, and the Midlands, as well as General American (also known as 'Good American'), various bits of Europe, and a fairly solid go at an Australian accent that would probably make most Antipodean stomachs churn but which was good enough to put on a CV in Britain.

Being able to put on different accents was a relatively rare skill, and it became a minor competition among my peer group to see how many you could legitimately put on your CV, a demonstration of vocal versatility that would, we believed, wildly broaden our potential casting opportunities.[*]

The price for the demo reel seemed prohibitive, but in return you had someone write material to suit your voice's ability and range, and studio time to record and edit the reel. At the end of the session you were handed a professionally recorded and edited result. And the tape[†] came with a list of voice agents who were open to accepting unsolicited voice-over demos, and keen to expand their books. It was said, nay, whispered, that the first voice-over job would recoup all your initial outlay. So, as a gamble, it was at least marginally better than betting on the Grand National or hanging around outside the National Theatre with a 'Will Act for Money' sign.

I sent copies to six agents. A few days later, with two unceremoniously returned, I was starting to wonder whether my letter had backfired, which if memory serves ended with something like: 'In order to save you the trouble of replying to this letter, I will contact your office in seven days . . .'

Then my cell phone rang.

J – 'Ello, squire, this is Jane from [one of the best voice agents in town]. I couldn't be bothered to wait the week; want to come in for a meeting?

Trying not to sound too excited, I agreed to meet the next

---

[*] It didn't.

[†] Yes, tape. Not CD. Shush.

day in their Soho offices. Now, I know those streets inside out from all the voice-over work I've done, but back then it was still a bit of a mythological world to me.* I got lost trying to find their offices, (literally) bumped into the film director Mike Leigh on the way, and was not succeeding in trying to be coy when I finally did get to the meeting and the wonderful Jane ended her introductory speech with the words:

J – Well, son, we're in if you are.

Flustered by the directness, and having been schooled to play the game, I explained I couldn't give a definite answer, as I had other agents to meet, said thank you, and staggered out. I wandered down the street in a daze, stopped, gave myself a metaphorical slap and called Jane immediately:

– Screw the other meeting. I like you; I want in.

Over the following days I received a stream of questions demanding to know the accents, character-types, and languages I could do. Combined with the skills I'd demonstrated on my reel, Jane was now armed to target those jobs to which I'd be best suited.

Now, having grown up in Wales, being grudgingly taught Welsh (as a non-native English boy) and having studied French to the end of High School, both Welsh and French were some of the languages I had proclaimed to be fluent in.

Brazenly, and foolishly, it seems. My cell phone rang.

J – You've got Welsh down. Are you fluent?

---

* I always think it's odd that Soho is best known as London's red-light district: for every door leading to a dimly lit, red-neon stairway, there are five behind which lurk recording studios, post-production film studios, and agencies. Their percentage is the same though.

– Sure, I said, having being taught in drama school never to say no.

J – Good, because you've got your first voice-over tomorrow: an advert for the post office. In Welsh. Good luck. Ha!

– . . . Fine, I gulped. Was that a laugh? I'd never find out. She'd hung up anyway.

I should probably take a moment to clarify that which I had failed to entirely make clear on my CV: while I understood a *lot* of the Welsh language, my chief ability to date was the school-ground test of correctly pronouncing the name of a small town in Anglesey:

Llanfairpwllgwyngyllgogerychwyrndrobwllllantysiliogogo-goch. [*]

But I could also say – and I was rather proud about this one,

Rydw yn hoffi coffi. [†]

Nevertheless, I still thought I could wing it by reading the script phonetically. My plan was perfect apart from two vital flaws: firstly, you rarely ever get the script ahead of the recording session, and secondly, unbeknownst to me as I sat down in front of the microphone that first time, copywriters rarely write exactly twenty-nine seconds of material (half a second of silence tops and tails each advert in a sequence of thirty-second commercials). I managed to make the script intelligible, but no matter how quickly I flipped and twisted

---

[*] St Mary's Church in the hollow of the white hazel near to the rapid whirlpool of Llantysilio of the red cave.

[†] I like coffee.

my tongue around the familiar-yet-foreign sounds of Welsh, we always ended up with forty-five seconds of material. I was asked if I could edit the script down, being fluent in Welsh and all, and I distinctly remember a bizarre gravitational pull drawing me underneath the desk to hide.

Fortunately, neither the client nor the sound engineer could speak Welsh either. To this day I have no idea what I said, but it was most definitely in a very good Welsh accent, and I believe the Welsh post office thrived.

In celebration of our years together, I met Jane for lunch while writing this book. I asked her about the way in which the tide had turned away from RP.

J – Well, it used to be that if you had a brown, rich, deep voice, you were money. People wanted to hear their mother's doctor or the local vicar, but it all started to change in 2000. From then on, the preference switched to natural, regional voices – *comfortable* was the key – and I think it was the economy that did it.

Suddenly there was less money around, and clients needed to get *exactly* the right voice, recorded in the *smallest* amount of time, and for that voice to hit *exactly* the right frequency to encourage the *maximum* number of people to part with what *little* cash they had, suddenly finding themselves in the middle of a recession.

We weren't being asked for voices that were rich and brown any more; clients were asking for younger, less threatening, more accessible, more regional voices. *Chummy* and *natural* were the qualities we kept hearing over and over when people phoned up.

About a year later, Huw Edwards became the lead news anchor on the BBC. Again, a deep, rich voice but this time balanced with his native south Walian tones, and that's when we knew we were into a different game.

The reason David Dimbleby, Jon Snow, and Jeremy Paxman are at the forefront of the British political television media circus is precisely because they sound Establishment. Rather than the common man criticizing the well-spoken, RP faces off with RP. So while the actors who could slip through six different parts of the country without taking breath were once the turn, they'd still arrive speaking in RP and wouldn't admit to having a regional accent unless they were asked to.

Ian McKellen was part of the sea change when he guest-starred in *Coronation Street*. Everyone's eyebrows went through the roof, because they'd only ever heard this theatrical knight speak in that wonderful, rich, deep voice. Remember, even as Gandalf he stayed relatively RP. But he's from Burnley, in Lancashire, and when he used his broad native accent the general populace, who had never heard him *not* do RP before, loved it . . .

Jane paused. Took a sip of her vodka martini.

I asked whether it had changed the way she ran her books, opened up her lists because now she needed one actor for every major accent in the country?

More than that: having an accent is now part of the USP. When I'm asked for a Cumbrian accent I can fire back, 'Well, what *part* of Cumbria are you looking for?' Regional accents are considered less bland, less uniform; listeners' ears perk up, and you've *got* to make people *listen* more – at least that's what the advertisers are hoping for, at any rate.

Jane takes another sip, and blows menthol smoke into the air. I am rapt.

J – Think about *Four Weddings and a Funeral* for a minute.

I do. 1994. Hugh Grant. Sheep jokes. Is it still raining? I hadn't noticed. The breakthrough movie for Richard Curtis, and very much the forefather of the international success of *Notting Hill* in 1999. All full of privileged central London types who don't seem to do any real work, mainly because they're too busy agonizing over matters of the heart. Loved it.

J – Exactly. And everybody in that movie spoke in RP. BUT – John Hannah – remember, when Simon Callow's character dies, and Hannah reads Auden's 'Stop all the clocks . . .' at the funeral, he does it in his south-central Scottish brogue, and YES it's the most moving part of the story, and YES theirs is arguably the most moving relationship . . .

[*sip, drag, blow*]

. . . But the fact that he does it in the MOST beautiful, easy-to-hear, glorious Scots accent is startling in a way that Hugh Grant couldn't be with his foppish RP – and now Hannah is the voice of one of the biggest UK supermarket advertising campaigns.

B – So do you get many RP requests now? I was having fun quizzing the woman who gets me so much of my work – in ten years of working together I've never had a chance to ask her these questions.

J – Ahhh. Rarity! The requests are, nine times out of ten, 'Nice. Normal. Natural. Doesn't-sound-like-an-actor.'

– They mean RP?

J – Yeah.

– Ironic, considering how much time drama schools spend training their actors to nail down RP.

J – Oh, you still *have* to have RP, but only in the same way as you have to have passed a maths exam. No, most of the time I hear, 'London accent, please'. But that used to mean 'Cockney'. Now it can mean everyone, everywhere, from all across the world.

– Right? Don't they say there are around 400 languages in this city now?

J – Exactly. Unless you want Cockney East End, the Polish people that live here have a 'London' accent. The whole concept of what a London accent is has shifted and changed, mirroring the sea change of inhabitants. If we ever do get a request for RP, it's RP into Birmingham into Liverpool via Manchester in one line, please.

– So . . .

I look over my notes. In *The Times* early in 2014, a tutoring company was quoted as saying:

Rather than taking elocution lessons to speak the Queen's English, the trend has been towards individuals from diverse backgrounds wishing to adapt their voices for success in a surprising variety of contexts – sometimes even by sounding not posh.

The BBC newsreader Charlotte Green, once voted the 'most attractive female voice on national radio', has recently said, 'Received Pronunciation is on the wane . . . The BBC's days of employing people who sound like me are more or less over.'

Another person interviewed, a voice coach, said, 'I was brought up with a cut-glass accent and all my peers were the same . . . As I entered later teenage years and adulthood it became obvious that it was not always an advantage to speak well. It was therefore my first experiment to reduce my own accent. However, I am still able to use it.'

When a company called Trulawn (a rather brilliant name for purveyors of artificial grass) for some reason surveyed 1,000 people on their use of accents, 22 per cent said they had consciously changed their natural accent, 8 per cent had aimed to sound more posh and 4 per cent had tried to sound less posh.

The Times piece ended with a quote from another voice coach: 'A lot of people feel the accents that many in this present [Coalition] Government have can make them seem out of touch. It gives them an air of superiority that makes them seem impervious to other people's feelings. Interestingly, I have never had an inquiry or student who wanted to speak with Received Pronunciation.'

A voice-coach friend of mine had more practical reasons for not using her natural Scots. She said, 'I can't teach an American how to talk Australian if I'm talking in a Scottish voice. I need RP for a common ground.'

My mind drifts up from my notes, back to the bar; Jane is staring at me, still waiting for me to finish my sentence.

– . . . so – they're using RP as the base platform to explode off into the main regional sounds. Would you say the fall of RP, with the recession, changed the way we listen to things, changed the way we're sold things, and changed the association of what's trustworthy in a voice?

[*sip, drag, blow, sigh*]

J – I dunno, Ben. *You're* the writer.

I check my Twitter feed. A writer friend of mine had just posted: 'Flat vowels are our cultural heritage, Yorkshire people. Ordering a *grornday lartay* is a betrayal of everything we stand for.'

THE BBC AND THE 'POSH' RP

DAVID   When the BBC began broadcasting in the 1920s, its first director, John Reith, was very clear about its aims. The job of the new institution, he said, is 'to inform, educate, and entertain'. And to do this he felt it needed a voice that would be most widely understood – a 'common denominator of educated speech'. He chose, as I mentioned earlier, RP.

The decision was understandable and generally accepted, but it worried many people from the very beginning. In 1926, the *Daily Chronicle* expressed its anxieties:

> Is there not some danger that the uniform system of training in pronunciation as well as voice production, which the B.B.C. is planning, may lead to a tiresome and possibly infectious monotony of utterance? We see no reason why the B.B.C. should not rather cultivate a variety of accent, intonation and blend of sound, so long as each variety is good of its kind.

However, the occasional foray into the regions wasn't successful. In 1937 Charles Chilton (creator of the hugely popular 1950s radio series *Journey into Space* and *Riders of the Range*, as well as being the inspiration for *Oh! What a Lovely War*) began to present a programme of popular music, but listeners couldn't get on with his Cockney accent, and he was taken off the air.

During World War II BBC producers made a real effort to get regional accents heard in a wide range of programmes, such as talks, features, and comedy shows (such as *ITMA*). It was part of a broader strategy to foster national unity during wartime: the more people could be heard from all regions and backgrounds, it was felt, the more pride people would take in their regional diversity. Shakespeare did the same thing in portraying Wales, Scotland, Ireland, and England as united against the French in *Henry V*.

The strategy was controversial. During the early part of World War II, the Yorkshire broadcaster Wilfred Pickles was asked to read the national news. According to the broadcaster John Snagge, the idea came from Brendan Bracken, the Minister of Information, who gave two reasons:

> He suggests a change of voice as he feels listeners are getting a little tired of the so-called Oxford accent . . .

That supported the *Daily Chronicle*'s view. But the second reason was novel:

> . . . and as a security measure because your accent might not be so easily copied by the Germans.

He might have added a third reason, judging by the letters of praise Pickles later received from all over the country:

> The lads from Leeds and Manchester and all points north, south, east and west of those cities where the short 'a' was

part of the dialect found my voice brought them a comforting feeling that the old familiar places and faces were still there.

They especially loved his ending of the midnight news – *Good night*, followed by *Good neet*.

But the decision caused headline news in the national press, with Pickles' 'short *a*' repeatedly picked upon: *Lahst a Thing of the Pahst,* said one. Although the BBC's Listener Research Department found his reading to be surprisingly popular, even in the south of England, Pickles recalls that 'the abuse poured into the postal section of the B.B.C.'. People (other than the Germans) complained that they were unable to believe the news, read in such an accent. He rather enjoyed the fuss, but eventually decided to drop London-based news-reading and return to broadcasting up north, going on to present a hugely popular quiz show called *Have a Go*. In the news, RP became universal again.

In his autobiography, written in 1949, Pickles has a para-graph which is one of the most powerful statements in support of accent diversity I have ever read. It deserves to be reproduced in full, as it is prescient in anticipating how things would change a generation later:

> While I have the greatest respect for the many achieve-ments of the B.B.C., I believe they are guilty of the offence of trying to teach Great Britain to talk standard English. How terrible it is to think that we may some day lose that lovely soft Devonshire accent or the bluff and very wonderful Scots brogue or the amusing flatness and

forthrightness of the North-countryman's speech, or the music of the Welsh voice. May it be forbidden that we should ever speak like B.B.C. announcers, for our rich contrast of voices is a vocal tapestry of great beauty and incalculable value, handed down to us by our forefathers. Our dialects are reminders of the permanence of things in these islands of ours, where folks talk differently in places only five miles apart, a phenomenon that has its roots in the times when it took many days to ride from London to York by stage coach. Some countries have grown up at fifty miles an hour in an age of radio and telephones – but not ours, thank goodness.

Accents did retain a radio presence, but only in drama, comedy, soaps, and other 'light entertainment' settings – what we would today call 'reality' broadcasting. *Have a Go* went all over the country, and people loved its accent diversity. Comedy programmes used characters with strong regional accents, as we saw with Birmingham. And there was the most successful of all accent programmes of the post-war era: *The Archers* – 'an everyday story of country folk' – which began with a pilot programme in 1950 and launched in January 1951. It had 20 million listeners within five years.

Between 1950 and 1980, RP continued to be the official voice of the BBC, through its continuity presenters and newsreaders. Then, in 1980, it tried again, letting Dundee-born Susan Rae present on Radio 4. It was a short-lived experiment. Once again, letters of complaint swayed the powers that be, and she was moved to other duties. It was 1937 and

Charles Chilton all over again. But twenty-five years later, in 2005, the BBC devoted an entire week in August to celebrating the accents and dialects of the UK in its *Voices* project, and accent-colourings were everywhere. RP was still strongly present in continuity, news, weather forecasting, chat shows, and other flagship programmes, but so were Scottish, Welsh, Northern, Estuary, and other accent colourings. Susan Rae was back reading the news. What had happened to cause such a sea-change in attitude?

Local broadcasting and after

In a phrase: local radio. Attitudes began to change dramatically following the emergence of regional broadcasting stations around the UK. The vision behind this initiative, as expressed by the pioneer of local radio at the BBC, former war correspondent Frank Gillard, was 'to present on the air, and in many different forms and through a multitude of local voices, the running serial story of local life in all its aspects'. Aware of the success of pirate radio stations around Britain, in 1967–8 the BBC chose eight locations for an initial experiment: Radio Leicester, Sheffield, Merseyside, Nottingham, Brighton, Stoke-on-Trent, Leeds, and Durham. It took a while to build audiences: it was difficult to publicize what was on offer, and the stations were available only on VHF at the time. But the experiment was a success, and in 1969 the BBC made local radio a permanent fixture and created twelve more stations.

Then, in 1973, the newly formed Independent Broadcasting Authority (IBA) began licensing a fresh wave of commercial radio stations – over eighty within fifteen years. Two years later, Radio Ulster began broadcasting, and three years after that Radio Scotland and Radio Wales. In all cases, the dominant impression the new stations conveyed was the 'multitude of local voices'. And this diversity was reinforced by television, which brought everyday life into homes in a way that radio was never able to do – notwithstanding the success of *The Archers*. Granada television launched *Coronation Street* in 1960, with its accent focus reflecting city life in the industrial North of England. Viewing figures reached 20 million in less than two years. Other regional soaps quickly followed, from both the BBC and ITV.

Over half the famous sitcom series of the 1960s and 70s relied on accent diversity for their characters, or exploited the contrast between regional accents and RP. Following early series such as *The Larkins* (1958), the sixties' offerings included *Bootsie and Snudge* (1960–3), *Steptoe and Son* (1962–74), *The Likely Lads* (1964–6), *Till Death Us Do Part* (1965–75), and *Dad's Army* (1968–77). The seventies included *Last of the Summer Wine* (1973–2010), *Porridge* (1974–7), *It Ain't Half Hot Mum* (1974–81), and *Citizen Smith* (1977–80). Accent variation and satire was at the heart of *Monty Python* (1969–83). And regional voices coloured the major light entertainment shows, too. According to a writer in the *Daily Mail*, Liverpudlian Cilla Black was 'the real voice of the swinging sixties' and her Saturday night shows 'made regional accents on telly seem normal'. Terry

Wogan performed a similar role on BBC Radio 2 with his breakfast show (1972–84), and went on to make his Irish accent one of the best-known on television, in such annual events as *Children in Need* and *The Eurovision Song Contest*.

Commercial television had already come to the same conclusion. The contrast in use of accents is immediately apparent to anyone watching archive footage of commercials, where the plummy RP voices of ladies talking about washing powder or gentlemen praising cars are one of the most noticeable features. Today, RP is rare in ads, as Ben's voice agent confirms. Advertisers want warm and friendly voices, and look to the regions to provide them. At the same time they have to be careful. If the accent is too broad, it can be hard to understand and so defeat the purpose of the exercise. Also, care has to be taken not to exaggerate an accent, or push it into your ears, which can lead to negative publicity – as happened with the heavily accented Birmingham 'Anything for yow, cupcake' catchphrase in ads for Hotels4u in 2013. Most ads are more subtle – and the fact remains that the vast majority on British TV use regional voices.

Businesses have also come to appreciate regional accents. The mantra these days is that people interacting with the public need to be 'customer friendly', and RP is widely considered to be 'too posh'. Receptionists, telephone operators, and call-centre staff are the front line here, and it is noticeable how regional accents dominate. A phone enquiry about mortgages, car insurance, travel schedules, and a host of other products is likely to be answered with an accent that is ranked high for pleasantness (we'll talk more about this later), such as Edinburgh Scots or Yorkshire. The trend towards the outsourcing of call centres to India, very strong in the early 2000s, seems now to be reversing, following complaints about difficulties in understanding Indian accents – though my impression is that the problems were as often to do with dislike of the accent rather than a genuine problem of comprehension.

All this was being noted by senior management at the BBC and by politicians. In the 1970s a committee chaired by Lord Annan was formed to report on the future of broadcasting. Part of its brief was to recommend a system that better reflected the political and cultural diversity of the UK. When it reported in 1977, one of its views was, 'We welcome regional accents'. The climate was right for the eventual creation of the *Voices* project I mentioned earlier. And the ripples created by that project continued, reinforced by complaints from licence-fee payers that the BBC was ignoring large parts of the country by failing to employ people with regional accents. In 2008, the BBC's director-general Mark Thompson agreed that 'we could hear a broader variety of English accents across our output', and hoped that the impending move to Manchester would help. But the story isn't over yet. Every now and then there is a press report saying that a radio or TV presenter has been 'sacked' because of their accent – though it's always difficult to know if the voice was really the main issue. However, the climate has definitely changed. All channels display regional voices now – even the upmarket BBC Radio 3. Listen to Ian McMillan and his Yorkshire-toned weekly, *The Verb*. Inconceivable twenty years ago.

Can you tell – in England?

DAVID Thanks to the diverse origins and multifarious influences on English over the past 1,500 years, there are more accents per head of population in the British Isles than in any other part of the English-speaking world. As I said earlier, travelling around the populated parts of England, I hear a noticeable accent shift every twenty-five miles or so – sometimes much less. A town like Welshpool, on the Wales/England border, is a good example of an accent contrast within a short distance. When I was exploring this part of the country for a television documentary as part of the BBC *Voices* project, I met people living to the east of the town, looking towards England, who sounded their *r*s after a vowel (as in *car* and *farm*) in a way that was similar to what is heard further south in Gloucestershire. The people I met living to the west of the town didn't do it. Their accent sounded much more Welsh. And there was only five miles or so between them.

With so many traditional accents to deal with, and so much mobility and migration (resulting in mixed accents), it's no longer possible to generalize about any part of the country. We can never say that 'everyone in Yorkshire' or 'everyone in Liverpool' has the same accent. But it is possible to identify a few general features that are used by most people in a particular area. They're especially noticeable when people speak with a 'broad' or 'strong' accent, so I'll focus on these in the selection of places below.

North vs south

Probably everyone knows that England divides into two main accent areas, north and south, though the boundary line between the two, somewhere in the South Midlands, isn't so easy to define. There are two main distinguishing features.

- The vowel in such words as *up* and *but* is rounded in the north ('oop') but not in the south ('ahp'). That means *but* rhymes with *put* in the north, but not in the south.

- The vowel in words like *bath* is short in the north and long ('bahth') in the south.

It's not so easy to divide up the rest of England. There's no simple division between east and west that applies to the whole country. In the north, the Pennines form a natural barrier which has made speakers to the west (Lancashire, Cumbria) sound different from speakers to the east (Yorkshire, Durham, Northumberland). But further south, the boundaries aren't so clear. There's certainly a big difference between people from the West Midlands and East Midlands, but there's a spectrum of accents across the area. And in the south, where the country is widest, there are even bigger differences.

Listening to the way people speak across southern England, we need to distinguish at least four major dialect areas. In the far south-west, Cornwall and Devon. In the central south-west, Somerset, Dorset, and Wiltshire, along with western parts of

Oxfordshire and Hampshire. In the south-east, the rest of Oxfordshire and Hampshire, along with all the 'Home Counties' – Berkshire, Sussex, Surrey, Kent, Essex, Hertfordshire, Bucking-hamshire – and much of Bedfordshire, Cambridgeshire, and Northamptonshire. In the east, East Anglia – Norfolk and Suffolk, along with parts of the nearby eastern and southern counties.

The other big factor is to do with the major cities. The simple presence of large numbers of people with different regional histories generates a complex accent mix. Throughout the history of Britain since the Middle Ages, we see people travelling to the cities to find work. Influences from abroad are important, especially in the capital and in the coastal cities. We find multiple accents in any urban centre, but the mix is especially noticeable in places like London, Birmingham, Liverpool, Manchester, Bristol, Hull, and Newcastle, and as a result of the continual mixing we find accent features that are very different from the rest of the region in which the city falls. There are big differences, for example, between Liverpool and the surrounding Lancashire, or Newcastle and the surrounding Northumberland.

The West Country

This isn't a very well-defined area, but it's usually taken to mean the counties from Herefordshire in the north, down to the south coast and the counties further west. Cornwall, Devon, Somerset, Dorset, and Gloucestershire are definitely 'West Country'. Wilt-shire, Oxfordshire, Berkshire and Hampshire display more of a mix, looking linguistically east as well as west.

- The main feature is that *r* is pronounced after vowels in words like *car* and *farm*. This used to be a characteristic of the whole country – it was a noticeable feature of pronunciation in Shakespeare's time – and of course it travelled across the Atlantic to America. It's still strongly present in the south-west, but it's much less likely to be heard in the counties to the east these days. Nowhere else in England uses it, apart from a sporadic presence in Central Lancashire, so it's a really important marker of identity. As Ben said earlier, the world of cinema pirates, from Robert Newton to Geoffrey Rush, make great use of it.

- The further west we go, the more we're likely to hear words like *so* and *from* pronounced with a voiced initial consonant – *zo* and *vrom*. It's a feature that has been in the area for some time. Shakespeare has Edgar in *King Lear* use a disguised West-Country accent, containing words like *vortnight* and *zir*.

The north-west – but not the far north-west

This is an area that runs from Birmingham up through the West Midlands, and into Cheshire, Merseyside, and Central Lancashire, with the eastern boundary running down through Nottingham-shire and Derbyshire.

- An important feature is that the *g* is pronounced in words like *sing* and *wrong*. That means people from this part of England will rhyme *singer* with *finger*. The large populations of Liverpool, Manchester, and Birmingham (locals say 'Birming-gum') makes this a frequently encountered pronunciation.

The east and south Midlands and East Anglia

This area runs from southern Lincolnshire down through eastern Leicestershire and Northamptonshire and across through north-ern Bedfordshire into Essex. It chiefly includes Norfolk, Suffolk, and Cambridgeshire.

- Words like *few* and *beautiful* drop the *y* sound after the initial consonant, so that the 'fyoo' of RP is heard as 'foo'. The nation as a whole heard this some years ago when a TV advertisement for poultry from Norfolk described the produce from the area as 'bootiful'.

- Words like *beer* and *here* have a more open start to the diphthong, so that they take on the quality of the vowels heard in *bare* and *hair*. Someone with a Norfolk accent would rhyme *here* and *there*.

The central Midlands and the north

This area runs from Staffordshire and Leicestershire north to the Scottish border, taking in the whole of Lancashire, Yorkshire, Cumbria, Durham, and Northumberland.

- An important feature is the way people say the final vowel in words like *funny* and *pity*. In other parts of the country, we hear an '-ee' ending: 'funnee'. The two vowels in a word like *weedy* are the same. But in this area, the vowel is short – sometimes like the *i* in *sit* (in which case the two vowels in *pity* would sound the same) and sometimes like the *e* in *set* (the two vowels in *Betty* would sound the same).

What's interesting is that this features isn't strongly present in Newcastle and its hinterland, or in the area around Liverpool. Nor is it noticeable in the area around Hull. People in the coastal cities for some reason tend to keep the 'ee' sound in these words.

The far north

This area includes both sides of the Pennines, from Central Lancashire and south Yorkshire up to the Scottish border.

- Words like *late* and *make* have a diphthong in RP, but in this part of England the vowel has lost its double quality, coming out as a long or short *e*. It's difficult to capture the sound in spelling, but a form like 'mehk' or 'mairk' (without the *r* being pronounced) hints at the long vowel, and 'mek' the short one. This is one of the big unifying features that distinguishes the Midlands from the north.

The south-east

RP is the accent traditionally associated with the Home Counties and London, though the mixed accent called 'Estuary

English' (we'll talk about this later) is now widespread. Among the most noticeable features of RP are the following.

- The *r* is not pronounced after a vowel, so we hear 'cah' for *car* or 'fahm' for *farm*.

- The vowel in words like *bath* is long – 'bahth'.

- The vowel in words like *cup* is quite open, lacking the lip-rounded or central (*the*-like) quality heard elsewhere. Outsiders sometimes mishear *cup* as *cap*.

- The vowel in words like *man* is made towards the front of the mouth, lacking the central or back quality heard in other accents. Outsiders sometimes mishear *man* as *men*.

- Initial *h* is always pronounced – unlike in most other regional accents in England.

IN THE CITIES

Newcastle

Broad Tyneside speech – or 'Geordie', as it's usually called (an adaptation of *George*) – is one of the most distinctive accents of England, thanks mainly to the way it uses diphthongs in a different way from RP and other accents. The accent has changed a lot in the past century. In particular, it has largely lost the *r* sound made not with the tip of the tongue, as in other accents, but with the back of the tongue against the uvula – similar to the *r* often heard in French. It was called the 'Northumbrian burr'. It seems to have died out now, though it's still occasionally heard in the speech of older speakers.

- Words like *make* and *coat* keep their diphthongs, but the second element goes in a different direction from what we hear in RP. Whereas RP sounds *make* as 'may-eek', Geordie sounds it more like 'may-uhk'. Similarly, *coat* comes out not like 'coh-oot' but as 'coh-uht'.

- A *y* sound is often inserted before a vowel, so that table comes out as 'tyeble' and home as 'hyem'.

- Words such as *work* and *firm* come out as 'wawk' and 'fawm', which is a major source of confusion for speakers of other accents. 'Mike can't work' is likely to be interpreted by an outsider as 'Mike can't walk'.

- So what happens to *walk*? This uses the 'ah' vowel we hear in RP *bath*. It's a sound that is heard in any word that has a spelling where *a* is followed by *l*. *All*, for instance, is pronounced 'ahll'. It's an ancient pronunciation, lost in RP – but very much present in Shakespeare's day.

Liverpool

This city and its hinterland has an interesting mix of features, reflecting its geographical location in north-west England and its history of immigration from Ireland in the nineteenth century. The Liverpool accent – 'Scouse', as it is usually called (an abbreviation of the sailor's dish, lobscouse) – is very different from the other accents of Lancashire. As well as the 'ee' feature already noted, we hear the following.

- Words like *hair* and *her* are identical. *Fair hair* comes out as 'fur ur' – and this spelling is widely used in attempts to write Scouse down, such as *thur* ('there') and *whur* ('where'). It's the basis of a great deal of wordplay, such as 'Him and Hair' (the name of a hairdressing salon).

- The Irish connection is recalled in the replacement of the *th* in words like *this* and *there* by a *d* – 'dis', 'dere'.

- Words containing the sounds *p, t,* or *k* are strongly aspirated, so much so that the sounds change their character completely, taking on a hissy character. The friction is especially noticeable at the end of such words as *like* or *look*, where the effect is very similar to the *ch* at the end of Scottish *loch*. Another Irish connection, especially with Dublin.

- The long 'oo' vowel in words such as *moon* and *Liverpool* comes out as a diphthong, with the first element like a short 'ee'. So the local pronunciation of the city name is 'Liverpiwl'.

Bristol

The noticeable feature here is the insertion of a final *l* after words that end in a vowel (usually spelled *a*), such as *India*, *Pamela*, and *IKEA*. This means that there's no difference between such word-pairs as *area* and *aerial*, *idea* and *ideal*, or *drawing* and *drawling*.

Birmingham

As well as using a short *a* in *bath*, a rounded *u* in *cup* and a sounded *g* in *sing* (see above), we find a number of distinctive features, some of which will be heard in other parts of the West Midlands, but with slightly different qualities.

- The diphthong in words like *float* has a much more open onset, so that it sounds more like RP *flout*.

- The diphthong in words like *nice* begins with a back and rounded quality, so that it sounds like 'noice'.

- The diphthong in words like *loud* begins with a front and higher quality, so that it sounds more like 'le-ood'.

- The vowel at the end of words like *sorry* is a diphthong, so that it sounds more like 'sorr-uh-ee'. This is another feature of the pronunciation of Shakespeare's time.

London (Cockney)

Some of the features associated with traditional Cockney have disappeared, such as the replacement of *v* by *w* or *w* by *v* seen in the way Charles Dickens made some of his characters speak – *Samuel* as *Samivel* and *vittles* as *wittles*. But Cockney remains one of the most distinctive accents in Britain, mainly because several consonants are affected as well as vowels.

- The *t* in the middle of words is replaced by a glottal stop, so that *Waterloo* and *bottle* become 'Wa'erloo' and 'bo'le'. The *t* at the end of a word is replaced too, so that *hot* become 'ho" – a feature that has spread into Estuary English.

- The *h* before a vowel is dropped, so that *hill* becomes ''ill'. An *h* may be inserted before a vowel, especially in emphatic speech, so that *arm* becomes 'harm'.

- The *th* sounds of RP are replaced by *f* and *v*, so that Cockneys don't distinguish between *fin* and *thin* or *than* and *van*.

- An *l* after a vowel sounds like a vowel, so that *people* comes out more like 'peep-ow'.

- Words like *tune* lose the *y* sound heard in RP after the first consonant, so that 'tyoon' comes out as 'toon' (as in American English).

- The diphthong in words like *make* sounds like the one in RP *Mike*. This is a famous sound, thanks largely to the way Professor Higgins trains Eliza Dolittle (in *Pygmalion/My Fair Lady*) to say 'The rain in Spain falls mainly on the plain'.

- The diphthongs in words like *now* and *town* have varying pronunciations. Some speakers make them further forward in the mouth, in the direction of the vowel in RP *men* – 'ne-oo', 'te-oon'. Others replace them with a single long open vowel – 'nah', 'tahn'. This is another famous elocution exercise when teaching someone to speak RP: 'How now, brown cow.'

- Words like *see* have a diphthong with a central start, so that they come out as 'suh-ee'.

- Words like *time* have a start further back in the mouth, and are rounded, so that they come out like 'toime'.

- Words that end with an unstressed 'uh', as in *copper*, are heard with a more open sound, more like 'coppa'.

A SCOTTISH PLAYER

BEN

Hilton – Yeah, that's a good question . . . When I was at university, [assumes RP] the George Square University, in the summer holiday, we did, err . . . *The Flies – Les Mouches –* in which Ian Charleson and I were both up to play the lead, Orestes. And they cast *me*, which was sensational, and Ian played Zeus. I had *no* idea what I was doing. Absolutely no idea. Seriously, I really was learning how to act, live on stage. A friend came to see it, and said, 'All I can see you doing is listening to the sound of your voice.' Because I was trying so hard to get rid of my Scots.

Hilton McRae and I were sitting outside a cafe in north London, drinking coffee. We'd been friends and colleagues for years, and I'd never asked him about his accent and his career before.

– Why get rid of it?

H – Because I thought that was what I had to do, to do classical theatre. I was only twenty, twenty-one.

– So what did you do?

H – I was so . . . I really didn't know what I was doing. I

don't think I did anything. But then jump to a few years later, and I was doing a workshop on *King Lear*. I was playing Edmund. In the middle of it all, I auditioned for Trevor Nunn at the Royal Shakespeare Company. So I did the Bastard speech [from the opening of Act 1, Scene 2] in RP.

> Why bastard? wherefore base?
> When my dimensions are as well compact,
> My mind as generous, and my shape as true,
> As honest madam's issue? Why brand they us
> With base? With baseness? Bastardy? Base, base?
> Who, in the lusty stealth of nature, take
> More composition and fierce quality
> Than doth, within a dull, stale, tired bed,
> Go to the creating a whole tribe of fops,
> Got 'tween asleep and wake? Well, then,
> Legitimate Edgar, I must have your land:
> Our father's love is to the bastard Edmund
> As to the legitimate: fine word, – legitimate!
> Well, my legitimate, if this letter speed,
> And my invention thrive, Edmund the base
> Shall top the legitimate. I grow; I prosper:
> Now, gods, stand up for bastards!

I finished, he came over, and he Trevv'd me [put his arm around Hilton, and half-hugged as he gave his notes], then said,

TN – Where do you come from?

H – Dundee.

TN – OK, so do the speech again, but this time you're in a room in Dundee, with all the other bastards.

H – And I absolutely nailed it. It was like channelling a different source of energy altogether. The stiff, upright 'classic' RP Shakespeare read-through made me feel and sound, well, stiff and upright – legitimate! Whereas m'growling, brawling natural Scots tones immediately changed how I felt about who I was, and especially physically. It was a revelation. It released me, y'know?

Hilton sits back and squints in the sunlight. Hilt and I worked together on my first professional Shakespeare job. I was understudying his Feste in *Twelfth Night*. I met him at the read-through, walked over and, all excited, said,

– Hi, I'm understudying you!

And Hilt said,

– Oh God, you poor thing.

And walked away. It was a long gig, and we bonded over a love of the Bard.

The next year, I got an audition for a production at Shakespeare's Globe. I met the director at her home, and auditioned in her kitchen. I spoke the spear-carrier speech I'd been given in my finest RP. She cocked her head at me.

D – Where are you from?

– North Wales.

D – Can you still do a Welsh accent?

– Sure, I said, in the brogue of my home. – When I go home I speak like that, y'kno?

D – Do the speech in your Welsh voice, then.

I thought for a moment. In university, I spoke in the Welsh

language. Once. I was sitting outside, shivering, next to the beautiful Irish girl I was smitten with, as I pretended to do some revision.

– *Mae hi'n oer*, I said.

IG – No, you're not annoying me, she said, not looking up from her papers.

– What? No! I said, it's cold. In Welsh, I added weakly. I was used to being asked to speak the language from time to time. Or even put on the accent. I'd even been asked to speak Shakespeare in the Welsh language. But Shakespeare in the *accent* of my home was something I'd only ever tried practising by myself in a London park.

I stared at the floor in front of the director's feet. I summoned up thoughts of home, of hard coast, wind and rain . . .

I spoke the speech in my Welsh tones, I got the part, and I spent the next six months acting on the Globe stage, in that same Welsh accent: sixty or so performances, to 120,000 people over the course of the summer of 2005. It was an awesome experience. But I spoke it in an accent that people would notice as being different, left-field, an *unusual* accent to hear Shakespeare in.

I tell Hilt all this and he squints at me, smiling. Then in his lackadaisical Scottish drawl:

H – Exactly. So after that meeting with Trevor, I went back into rehearsal and did Edmund in my own voice, as it were. The guy producing the workshop, a Scots guy – I didn't really like him – came up *the day before we opened* and said, 'You're hiding behind that voice.' 'Ha! Thanks,' I muttered after him, or words to that effect . . . Sometimes you can't win. Hide behind RP or hide behind your natural voice? But I got into the RSC on that audition with Trev. It was 1977. Everything was great. Then I did a takeover [where a production changes cast but the show continues] of *Troilus and Cressida*. I was cast as – who's the lover of Cressida?

– Troilus?

H – No.

– Diomedes?

H – Yeah, Diomedes. Trevor had asked me to do Greg Hicks's part in *Macbeth* with Ian McKellen and everyone told me not to. One of my big mistakes.* So I did Diomedes, and everyone really egged me on to play it really Glaswegian. At the final run-through before we opened, the director called me over and said, 'Just so's you know, you'll get the worst reviews you've ever had.' And I did. So anytime I see Francesca Annis – who played Cressida – I apologize to her.

– Why?

H – Because I din't – I was stoopid; I didn't understand what Diomedes was *doing*, I just focused on the accent. I was a huge hit before that as Launcelot Gobbo in *Merchant of Venice*, but after *Troilus and Cressida* I walked into the casting office at the RSC to meet Peter Brook, to see about *Antony and Cleopatra*. The casting director had left out her casting notes and it said, *Failure as Diomed. Best at being Scots.*

---

* Judi Dench played Lady Macbeth; the show is considered one of the greatest Shakespeare productions of the twentieth century. A relatively large #HiltonFail, but he *was* in *Star Wars Episode VI*, so it kinda evens out.

– What do you do with that? When your accent is so much a part of your identity?

H – Scots or not, I was shite in a bottle. I just had no idea what it was to be an actor. It can *start* from there, but the accent can't be the only hook you hang your character hat on. If it is, everything you're doing is paper thin. The accent has to come *from* somewhere, from a *person*, it has to be *real*.

– So how do you perceive your accent now?

H – Ach, my accent is so weird. Since 1985, when I played Orlando in *As You Like It*, I've been acting with my 'natural voice'. Still, I've learnt it's *oven* instead of *ohven*. It might well be *bahth* but I know it's actually really *bath*. I know I've a hard *l* in my voice. But I don't care. The other side of that coin is if I get work in Scotland, especially in theatre, the Scots actors treat me like an English fool. They tell me my Scots accent is terrible.

– Talk about a rock and a hard place.

H – I mean it was so bad once I really had to hold on to myself a bit, you know. They're mean, those bastards.

– Because of the fierce nationalism?

H – Yeah. I'm a traitor. I've moved to London and tried to hide my roots – at least from their point of view. I attended a meeting on the state of Scots culture once. I stood up, said, 'I'm Hilton, I'm an actor, I live in London,' and the audience Boooooo'd me. They *booed* me. I din't say to hell with it but I should have. I hate that parochialism . . .

. . . So that was going on. But, yeah, I discovered in the early eighties I was pretty good at accents. Faultless Cockney. My American is pretty good. It *is* good. So, yeah, I've learned now – I just speak. In increasing years I pare away everything, everything, everything. I speak as I speak. I was warned about using my Scots, but it didn't matter. Hey, talking of which, when you saw me in *Weapons of Happiness* a few years ago, you asked me why I used my Scots accent.

– I did? I remember the play I saw you in a few months ago, about the Jewish secret police and the Palestinians locked up. Everyone used their own accents, which was OK, but it did jar slightly that a broad Glaswegian was playing opposite you as the head of the Jewish secret police.

I tell Hilton about my first film job, two years after leaving drama school. I was cast as a young member of the Jewish uprising in the Warsaw Ghetto, c.1942. You couldn't get more specific, accent-wise. An English script, but we had to reconstruct a Polish-Jewish accent from sixty years ago. I had two sessions with an accent coach in the middle of a very expensive, leafy part of north London, and spent time learning some Czech and Polish while we were out filming (ironically, in neighbouring Slovakia). When we were asked to re-record some dialogue back in London, after three months shooting in Europe, I had to say the line, *Yes, hurry*. But my accent was so keyed in, the *r*s were so thick they couldn't understand what I was saying any more. Schoolboy error, not sacrificing a touch of authenticity for a bucketload of intelligibility.

H – Exactly. And I was playing a Czech in *Weapons of Happiness*. You noticed that there was a slight inching towards the accent when I spoke to the audience, but the rest, when I was talking to anyone else, was just my natural voice. In the original production, the guy who played my part spent two months with Czech émigrés – with the result that no one understood what he was saying. It was correct, but it was ridiculous.

Hilt smiles, starts to roll a cigarette.

H – I got great reviews for Orlando, but I won't forget this one reviewer who described me as 'a Scots Mick Jagger lookalike'. But what's Scottish got to do with ANYTHING? It doesn't *matter*. It's like when actors get reviews like 'a pock-marked performance' because they've got bad skin. What's that got to do with *anything*? So now I *can't* do RP. Haven't tried. But I'm very confident in my art. My technique. That Leonard Bernstein quote, 'Don't get in the way of the words and the audience.'

– Is there a situation where you would use RP now?

H – No. I can't. Never would. *Don't* cast me in a Noël Coward play. I wouldn't want to do it. Don't understand these people. I wouldn't know what to do.

– Because . . . because the accent is too intrinsically linked to the fabric of their being?

H – Yeah. The *Private Lives* at the National Theatre a few years ago with Alan Rickman and Lindsay Duncan was so good. They got rid of the cut-glass accent. I saw a different production a few months later in Brighton; they used RP and I thought, Nobody cares. I don't care what you're saying to each other.

– So what did Alan and Lindsay do?

H – They just spoke as they speak.

– So, unless you're Noël Coward, don't do his plays?

H – It's just difficult because he wrote those parts for his voice, and no one talks like Coward.

– OK, so only RP speakers should do Coward?

H – It's definitely a more difficult job, without being of that certain class.

– Y'know, I still get emails from students at drama school that get told, 'Unless you speak RP you won't be cast in Shakespeare.'

H – They are mistaken beyond hugely. That's ridiculous.

– They're very confused and upset about it, flattening out their own sound.

H – I'm sorry, but if a play is set in Florence why use RP? Why can't I play a Florentine as well as [insert name of any well-known RP-speaking actor here]? What's that about? That has to be *stopped*.

– I mean, I get it, there are shapes I can't bend my mouth into, like Geordie. But I don't try to parrot the sound, I try to find a way into the psychology of the town, the place. I played a young Mancunian cop for a play a few years ago and went on a ride-along with the police so I could properly hear what I was supposed to be shooting for. Goodness knows if the audience noticed, but it gave me a depth to what I was saying, and the way I was saying it.

H – I like that about Original Pronunciation.[*] There's no place to set it to. I love OP.

– Why?

H – Because it gives a natural depth to the words. You really have to find the words inside you. It has an extraordinary resonance. More so than anything I know. But I do think that if we were to mount a full production in OP we'd have to

---

[*]   The reconstruction of Shakespeare's accent. We're coming to it . . .

take it back a bit, so it's never anything but *clear*. When it's unintelligible, *forget it*.

– I ran a workshop last year, and worked with this terrific young Scots actor. He had the richest, deepest, bass-bass voice, and I asked him to give a speech from *Macbeth*, the character of Lennox.

H – Yeah, well, if there's a part you do in Scottish, it's that one.

– Right. But he gave the speech in a beautiful, perfect RP. I said – like Trevor said to you – 'OK, great, now do it in your natural voice.' 'My Scots?' asked the young actor. 'Yep,' says I. 'But,' he said, bewildered, 'I've never spoken Shakespeare in my Scottish voice.' It staggered me that he was going through exactly what I'd experienced in my Globe audition. I pushed him to do it, he did, and it was so much more grounded, more heartfelt – it made so much more sense. When he finished, he looked up with tears in his eyes. He said, 'That was the most fantastic experience of my life.'

H – Exactly. And I'm not suggesting an actor should *only* do his accent, an actor should have loads of voices. But it has to be in the service of the words. If we accept Adrian Lester as *Henry V*,* surely we can accept that. At the Charleson Awards in 2013 there were fifteen nominees, and ten of them were non-Caucasian. It was fantastic. Why should only the few speak the best parts because of some age-old association?

---

* See 'The Rough and the Smooth', p. 56. Lester was the first black actor to play Henry V.

Can you tell – in the Celtic fringe?

DAVID   The regions of the British Isles where Celtic languages are spoken are Wales, Scotland, Ireland, the Isle of Man, and Cornwall. The fortunes of the Celtic languages in these areas have been very varied, with present-day efforts at revitalization yielding mixed results, but where there's a strong bilingual presence, the effect is immediately noticeable on speakers' English pronunciation. The distinctive features are in many cases of considerable age: the representation of a Scots accent, for example, can be traced back in literature to the early Middle Ages. As a result, Welsh, Scottish, and Irish accents are among the most recognizable of all the accents of the British Isles, with each region showing considerable variation. It's too soon to say what the long-term effects on English accents will be as a result of the resurgence of interest in Manx and Cornish, but if they follow the example of their Celtic cousins, one day the English spoken in the Isle of Man and Cornwall will be markedly different from what we hear today.

Someone from Scotland

As Hilton McRae (and Sean Connery) have emphasized, there are huge accent differences in Scotland. The bulk of the population lives in a large central lowland area running north-east to south-west roughly between Kincardine and Wigtown. It contains four main dialect areas, as well as the two big cities of Edinburgh in the east and Glasgow in the west, with their very different accents (listen to Maggie Smith as Jean Brodie vs Billy Connolly as himself). To the south, another cluster of accents distinguish the counties closest to England; and to the north a range of accents across the north-east and in the Highlands, where the influence of Scottish Gaelic is apparent. The Orkney and Shetland islands have an accent world of their own. But to anyone from outside Scotland, certain features stand out.

- The *r* after a vowel is always sounded, either as a flapped sound (as in RP 'very') or as a trill.

- Scottish speakers keep the old distinction, known in Old English but lost in RP, illustrated by *which* and *witch* or *whales* and *Wales*.

- They use the **ch** sound in words like *loch*, as well as in many dialect words, such as *richt* and *nicht* ('right', 'night').

- Scots tend to use a 'dark' *l* in all parts of a word, so that in words like *leap* the first consonant can make the word sound like 'luh-eep'.

- Several of the words distinguished by vowel length in RP sound the same in Scottish English. Pairs such as *full* and *fool* are identical, both with a short vowel. So are *Pam* and *palm*, and *cot* and *caught*.

- Many words that are lip-rounded in RP lose their rounding – *go* is often written as *gae*, *stone* as *stane*.

- Words with a high back vowel, as in *moon* and *use*, are

pronounced further forward in the mouth, but they keep the lip-rounding, so that the effect is a sound like the *u* in French *tu*.

- Words like *house* and *down*, which have a wide diphthong in RP, are pronounced as pure vowels, so that they are heard as 'hoose' and 'doon'. A parody of a Scottish accent often relies on this feature, as in 'There's a moose loose aboot this hoose' (used by Lord Rockingham's XI in 1958 in their number-one hit single, 'Hoots Mon').

- Words with a final unstressed syllable in RP often have it stressed in Scottish English, such as *SaturDAY* and *adverTISE*.

- Scots speakers tend to use a wider pitch range than in RP, especially at the ends of sentences, and the accent, like Welsh English, has sometimes been described as 'sing-song' as a result.

Someone from Northern Ireland

There isn't a sharp linguistic distinction at the border between Northern Ireland and the Republic of Ireland. The two types of accent merge into each other, with all kinds of mixtures being heard. But away from the border there are certain features that stand out, partly as a result of the history of the region, with the influence of the Scottish English of south-west Scotland an important factor (hence the often-used label, Ulster-Scots).

- The diphthong heard in such words as *late* has a starting point that is higher in the mouth, so that it comes out more like 'lee-uht'.

- The diphthong heard in words like *house* has a range of pronunciations, some of which are very noticeable to outsiders. Usually the first part of the diphthong is higher than in RP or Scots, so that it sounds more like the 'he' in *hen*. Many speakers also lip-round the first part of the diphthong as well as the second, so that it resembles the vowel in the French word *soeur*, 'sister'.

- Unlike Scottish English, people in Northern Ireland usually distinguish the vowels in pairs like *cot* and *caught*.

- The *r* after a vowel isn't usually flapped or trilled, as in Scotland, but has a quality much more like an American *r*.

- Again, unlike Scotland (but like Wales), the *l* in words like *peel* is 'clear'. In RP, the *l* sound at the beginning of a word is a different quality from the *l* sound at the end. Compare *leap* and *peel*: the latter sounds more like 'pee-uhl'. Technically, the *l* of *leap* is called a 'clear' *l*, and the *l* of *peel* is called a 'dark' *l*.

- Some vowel qualities are a long way from those heard in RP, so that outsiders can at times be confused. A joke illustrates. Mike is horrified to hear that John has joined a 'monastery', but is reassured when told that the job is actually for the government – at the 'Monastery of Education'.

Someone from the Republic of Ireland

Irish English – or Hiberno-English, as it's often called – is as varied in its accents as the other Celtic areas, but a number of features have been well captured by the writers of Ireland, often reflected in the spellings they use.

- The *r* after vowels is heard in words like *car* and *farm*.

- Irish speakers keep the distinction between *which* and *witch*, as in Scotland.

- The two *th* sounds of RP, as in *thin* and *this*, are replaced by *t*, so that *thanks* is heard as 'tanks' and *this* as 'dis'. The *t* and *d* also sound slightly different, being made with the tip of the tongue against the teeth rather than (as in RP) against the ridge above the top teeth.

- Words such as *tea* and *peacock* have a more open pronunciation than in RP, as seen in such spellings as *tay* and *paycock*.

- Words such as *join* and *boy* have a diphthong more like RP *my*, as seen in such spellings as *jine*.

- Words like *my* and *high* come out with the first element of the diphthong not so open, so we hear 'moy' and 'hoy'.

- Words like *many* and *any* have a more open sound, so that they come out like RP 'Manny' and 'Annie'. The same sort of vowel is also heard in words like *one* and *rock*.

- Words like *old* and *cold* have a more open start to the diphthong, sounding more like the diphthong in RP 'now'. Irish writing often spells them with an *ou* or *ow* (*the ould country*).

- Words with a long back *a* in RP (as in *calm* and *path*) are pronounced much further forward in the mouth. That long back sound *is* heard in Irish English, but in such words as *saw* and *talk*.

- Irish English speakers use the clear *l* in words like *full* and *field*.

- When speakers are influenced by Irish Gaelic, they often pronounce clusters of consonants in a Gaelic way, so that *stop*, for example, comes out as *shtop*.

- As in Scotland, many words have a stress at the end which would not be present in RP, as in *realISE*, *safeGUARD*, and *eduCATE*. This affects the word-endings too, so that Irish speakers will say that something is compli*cated*. It's noticeable especially in rhymes, such as *awaited* scanning with *elevated*.

Someone from Wales

There are big differences between the accents of North Wales and South Wales, and within these areas there are striking differences too. Bilingual speakers will display features of Welsh pronunciation more strongly, especially in the intonation of the voice. And certain areas show the marked influence of English accents, such as in the tourist resorts along the North Wales coast or in Pembrokeshire in the south-west (once called 'little England beyond Wales'). But some features are widely heard.

- Probably the most distinctive sounds are the two consonants that speakers from outside Wales find difficult, usually written *ll* and *ch*. The sound of the *ll* (as in *Llandudno*) is like the *l* sound in RP, but without any vocal cord vibration. People who can't manage it usually replace it with a *kl* – saying 'Klandudno'. They usually find the *ch* easier to pronounce, especially if they're familiar with Scottish *loch*, *och aye*, and other such words. If they can't manage it, they replace it with a *k*, as when the village of Chwilog in North Wales is pronounced 'Kwilog'.

- There's a strong tendency, especially in the south, to 'hold' a consonant between vowels, so that *honey*, for example, comes out like 'hun-nee', with a lengthened *n*, or *duty* comes out as 'dewt-tee', with a lengthened *t*.

- Welsh English speakers tend to use a clear *l* in all parts of a word.

- Unless there's been some influence from a regional accent of England, Welsh speakers don't pronounce *r* after a vowel (in *car*, *horse*, etc.). And when they do pronounce an *r* (as in *right*) it's often a flapped sound (as in RP *very*) or a trill.

- The central vowel, as in *the*, replaces the more open vowel heard in RP *cup*, *butter*, *trouble*, etc. So *butter*, for example, sounds like 'buht-tuh'. There's no lip-rounding, unlike in many parts of the north of England. On my *Voices* tour, I listened to a long-term (over forty years) resident of Rhyl whose accent was almost entirely Welsh. But he betrayed his northern English origins when he said words like *cup*, as they all had a rounded vowel.

- Words like *fire* and *sure* are just one syllable in RP – often like 'fah' and 'shaw'. In Welsh English, they are usually two: 'fi-yuh', shoo-wuh'.

- There's no *z* sound in Welsh, so words that would have this sound in RP come out with an *s* instead. 'Animalce' at a 'soo' might be very 'noicy'.

- An important feature is the melodic lilt of the voice, which is often described as 'sing-song'. What's happening is that sentences which in RP would end with a falling tone, are in Welsh English, often said with a rising tone, and when this tone is used high up in the voice, it can easily give an outsider the impression that the speaker is chanting.

SCONES, BISCUITS, AND *STAR WARS*

BEN 'Y'know, when you're in America,' an American friend of mine said while I was editing this chapter, 'when you're waiting tables, if someone comes in with an accent, you know you won't get tipped. Brits don't know how to tip. Y'all have butlers and valets and what-not, you should know. But yeah, accent equals stymied.'

One of the 'meals' British Airways gave me on the way over to Houston was a cup of tea, and a little packet within which was cream, jam, and a scone. The name of the cake was written on the neat little packaging. I used it as a sort of test as I travelled around the country. As the humble scone is the quintessential example of the accent divide in the UK, I wondered how the Americans I met would fare pronouncing the word. When I asked Thor, a northern Californian with Norwegian heritage, he, like most others I met, said *skonn*, to rhyme with 'one'.

TXC – Ah work dan on the EE-quator, said the Texan cowboy I was sitting next to.

I show him the packaging. Ask him what the word says.

TXC – That? That says *scohwn*. Why? We call 'em *biscuits*.

At the airport, it seems there's something wrong with my paperwork, and I listen to the beautiful Southern drawl of the immigration officers comparing websites on the best place to buy magazines. It's ten minutes into the conversation before I realize they're talking about harnesses, that they're talking about GUNS rather than *Hello!* or *Esquire*.

Two hours later, I step out of the fire and into the air-conditioned car of the teacher who's driving me to her school for the Shakespeare talk I'm going to give.

– So, what would you like me to talk about with your students?

T – Oh, anything you like, anything at all. But the parents pay a minimum of $20,000 per year so they kinda feel like they can call the shots.

– Oh-kayyyyy . . .

T – So just no bawdy. No swearing. No sex. And no . . . body parts.

This loosely translates to 'no Shakespeare'. If you were to remove any and all possible sexual references in the plays, you could write the remaining lines on a postage stamp. An awkward silence fills the sedan.

T – I eat egg white protein for lunch. I've been going to a Jungian dream councillor for two years. Do you meditate?

Houston, Texas, despite its passion for guns and apparent lack of tolerance for anything bare-flesh related, is the most culturally diverse state in the entire country. Quite the opposite of the stereotypical Southern hick image most associate with it.

We arrive at the school, which, despite being Greek

Orthodox Annunciation, is secular. I walk into the gym, where 400 ten-to-thirteen-year-olds have just tramped in. As I stand in the centre, I ask them to sit all around me, rather than me stand up on the stage and have them sit on the bleachers far away on the other side of the basketball court markings.

I give what I hope is an inspiring, funny, and passionate talk about Shakespeare. I deliver various speeches from the Bard's greatest plays, some in Original Pronunciation, getting deep into character as I draw from the well of the greatest words in the English theatrical canon. I enthuse greatly on the joys of acting Shakespeare, and encourage them to speak it to each other when they come to study it, and not just read it silently.

I draw to a close. There's a pause, a huge round of applause. It dies down. I say,

– So, do you have any questions?

A hundred hands shoot up. I point. A young student turns crimson, is nudged by a friend. I nod, equally trying to encourage. She summons up the courage, and says,

– Say 'banana'.

About to break into a Shakespeare-acting anecdote, I say,

– I was once – What?

Another voice shouts out:

– Say, 'tomato'.

The dam breaks:

– Say, 'I'm from Lahndon'.

– Give us your best US accent.

– Do Stewie from *Family Guy*.

– Caan yew tawk leyek thiis?

– Say, 'water'.

– Erm . . . Water?

400 voices – No, *watuh*!

Two weeks later, in Chicago, before I leave for the airport, I go to dinner with the actors I've been working with. Accents have been coming up a *lot*. Over here, Good American is the accent you're taught to speak Shakespeare with, and the actors I've met don't like it.

You've heard it a lot, probably without realizing it. It's a well-articulated, flattened American sound, distinct to no particular state, and if anything, lies somewhere halfway across the Atlantic, as it has a roundness that you'd associate with well-spoken RP. Think *Frasier*.

The restaurant we're having dinner at is slightly flamboyant, and there are a few puzzling words on the menu. One of my actors looks up, bemused.

A – Tartare . . . What is *that*?

– It's raw meat.

A – Oh.

– Ha. In Britain it's *goodbye*.

A – Oh. I didn't think you Brits actually pronounced your *r*s.

– We don't. It's *tah-tah*.

A – Oh.

– I was joking.

A – . . . Oh.

En route to the airport, and now slightly homesick after a

month on the road, we pass a sign that reads *Bryn Mawr Ave,* the name of a street in my home town in north Wales.

– Wow! Bryn Mawr Avenue.

A – Oh, we pronounce it *mar.*

– *Mawr* means *big.* We say *mao-wrrrrr.*

A – Oh. Yeah, we say *mar.*

I felt a twang of accent homesickness. For all my railing against RP, for all the associations, good and bad, that my various home accents give me, I've grown fond and bewildered in equal measure by the sounds I've heard over the last—

'Accent homesickness. That's a real thing, y'know,' says my American friend, reading over my shoulder. 'The voice on the Tube, y'know. You forget. And then when you go home, you hear your own voice again – on TV commercials, places, y'know?'

The plane lifts into the sky above Chicago, and I flip open the in-flight magazine. I read the following:

> On April 1, 2001, the manager of a Florida Hooters announced that the staffer who sold the most beer would win a Toyota. The winning waitress was led, blindfolded, to a . . . toy Yoda.

Can you tell – abroad?

DAVID It doesn't take long for an English accent in a new country to diverge from its point of origin. In the years following US independence, British travellers returning from a visit to the new nation were already commenting on 'the American accent' and talking about 'nasal twang' and suchlike. And over the course of a century we see not only the development of an accent that identifies people from a particular part of the English-speaking world, but also a range of accents within their countries, reflecting differences of age, gender, and social class. Nowhere quite matches the level of accent differentiation we encounter in the UK, but the notion that there are countries with no accent differences among its people is a complete myth.

Thanks to the media – especially cinema and television – most people are able to identify the English accent of a country other than their own in very general terms, calling it 'British', 'American', 'Australian', 'Irish', or whatever. Their ability usually breaks down, though, when asked to identify more specific accents within those countries. The differences between London, Liverpool, and Birmingham are as noticeable as the differences between New York, Boston, and Dallas, but few Americans would be able to distinguish the former, and few British the latter. The situation becomes even more difficult when listening to English speakers from countries which have never had the cinematic presence of a Crocodile Dundee to place their accent before the ears of the world.

Of course, one speaker does not make a nation. The problem with Crocodile Dundee, as I mentioned earlier, is that the accent used by Paul Hogan came to be identified as 'Australian'. Inevitably, listeners with no inside knowledge of Australia thought that all Australians talked like him. That was the equivalent of thinking that all British people speak like Cockneys or all Americans like Bugs Bunny. The point came up in my map-argument with Ben. There's a great deal of variation in Australia, with a spectrum of accents that at one end are conservative, cultured, and displaying a clear continuity with British English, and at the other end are broad, down-to-earth, and derive from the accents that the convict-settlers spoke. Lots of mixed accents in between, of course. A similar mix can be heard in Canada, New Zealand, South Africa, the Caribbean, India, and any country where English has come to be spoken by large numbers as a first or second language. So when we talk about identifying nations below, bear in mind that not everyone in these countries will speak in the same way.

How to tell a British speaker from an American

There are some regional accents in the two countries that have a great deal in common – which is hardly surprising, as British accents travelled across the Atlantic on the ships in the early seventeenth century. But when we compare the two prestige accents – RP and General American (GA) – there are several notable differences.

- RP has no *r* after a vowel, in such words as *car*, *heart*, and *farm*. GA does. (But in eastern New England, and much of the American South, people usually don't pronounce the *r* in these words.)

- RP has a long *a* vowel, formed towards the back of the mouth, in such words as *ask*, *bath*, and *half*. GA has a vowel much further forward, close to the quality heard when RP speakers say *man*.

- RP rounds the vowel in such words as *pot* and *hot*. GA doesn't, so that to a British listener, an American saying *hot* sounds more like a northern England version of *hat*.

- RP makes a clear difference between *t* and *d* between vowels, as in *writer* and *rider*. GA doesn't. The *t* is 'flapped', so that it sounds more like the *r* in a word like *very*.

- Many words have a different stress pattern, such as:.

  - In RP, *address*, *research*, and *weekend* have the stress on the second syllable. In GA it's on the first.

  - In RP, *garage*, *cafe*, and *ballet* have the stress on the first syllable. In GA it's on the second.

  - In RP, words ending in –*ary* or –*ory* (such as *secretary* and *laboratory*) don't have a stress on the ending. They do in GA.

  - This is one of the areas where American English is most noticeably influencing British English. GA stress patterns are increasingly heard in Britain. For anyone brought up on episodes of *Star Trek*, there's only one way of pronouncing *frontier*, and that's the American way, with the stress on *–tier*.

- Dozens of words follow no particular pattern, but are simply different. If you say *clerk* to rhyme with *park* you're following the British way. If you say it to rhyme with *lurk* you're identifying with America. *Route* rhyming with *boot*? British. Rhyming with *out*? American. *Vase* rhyming with *Ma's*? British. Rhyming with *days*? American. *Birmingham* ending with an unstressed syllable? British. Ending with a strong *–ham*? American. And similarly, *lieutenant* (beginning with *left* or *loot*), *herb* (with or without an *h*), *nougat* (with the *t* pronounced or not) . . . and of course, *tomato* and *schedule*, where this book began.

How to tell a Canadian from an American

Here too the influence of American pronunciation makes it difficult to generalize, especially among young people. But traditionally there are three big differences between GA and Canadian English.

- Most Canadians pronounce such pairs of words as *cot* and *caught*, or *collar* and *caller*, with the same short vowel.

- In words like *house*, *south*, and *out*, the beginning of the diphthong is formed higher in the mouth than in GA, with a quality like the *u* in RP *mud*. This is why Americans parody a Canadian accent by saying 'oot' for *out*. To British ears, the effect isn't so strange, as a similar quality (with *out* sounding more like *oat*) can be heard in many West Country or Irish accents.

- Similarly, Canadians use that central *mud*-like vowel in words like *fight*, *vice*, and *life*.

These last two features are technically called 'Canadian raising', and are the main sounds to listen out for.

How to tell an Australian from a Brit

The broad accent has shaped the popular image abroad, thanks to Crocodile Dundee, and to humour books such Afferbeck Lauder's *Let Stalk Strine* (= *Let's Talk Australian*).

- The title illustrates one of the main features of an Australian accent: the first part of the diphthong in words like *day*, *gate*, and *Australian* is much more open, more like the quality we hear in RP *I*. Lauder naughtily re-spells several words in this way, such as *ebb tide* ('appetite'), *tiger* ('take a') and *rye-wye* ('railway'). It's most often heard when Australians greet you with *g'day*, where the second syllable sounds more like 'die'. (Cockney speakers do the same thing, of course. It's one of the historical phonetic links with Britain.)

- The vowel in words like *bath* and *half* is much further forward than in RP.

- The vowel in words like *see* and *green* is a diphthong, with the first element like the vowel in unstressed *the*.

- The first part of the diphthong in words like *my* and *high* is made further back in the mouth than in RP, so that these words come out more like 'moy' and 'hoy'. (Several Irish accents do the same thing. Another historical link.)

- Where RP has an *i* sound in an unstressed syllable, as in *women* or *village*, Australians use the central vowel heard in *the*.

- And why do people talk of an 'Australian twang'? Because vowels that appear next to a nasal consonant (such as *down* and *now*) retain the nasality in the broad Australian accent much more than they do in RP.

How to tell a New Zealander from an Australian

The two accents are very close, as we'd expect, given the common history and frequent interaction between the two countries; but there are a couple of important differences.

- The main one, which Australians use a lot when parodying a NZ accent, is the way New Zealanders replace the high front vowel in words like *sit* and *fish* by a central vowel (like the *e* in unstressed *the*). So *fish and chips* becomes 'fush and chups'. (The parody works in the other direction too: New Zealanders have Australians saying 'feesh and cheeps'.) Ask an RP-speaker to say the name *Philip*, and we hear the two vowels sounding the same. Ask an Australian, and the second *i* sounds like the vowel in *the*: 'Phil-up'. Ask a

New Zealander, and both vowels have a *the*-quality: 'Phulup'.

- The vowel in words like *yes* and *get* is formed higher in the mouth than in Australian (which is already higher than it is in RP), so that these words sound more like 'yis' and 'git'. Similarly, the vowel of words like *mat* is higher up, in the direction of *e*, so that outsiders can mishear *mat* as *met*. I once got a name completely wrong. A man was introduced to me as *Jack*, but it came out as 'jek' and I interpreted it as *Jake*, thus naming him wrongly for quite a while.

How to tell a South African from a Brit

There's a wide range of accents here, reflecting the 'rainbow' character of the culture. At one extreme, some South African speakers have conservative accents that sound very like RP. At the other, there are accents strongly influenced by Afrikaans or by one of the various African languages spoken in the country.

- The raising of *a* and *e* vowels, heard in New Zealand, is found in South Africa too, so *pat* sounds more like RP *pet* and *pet* more like RP *pit*. There's an old witticism which is actually quite useful to outsiders who want to fix this pair of changes in their ears. For South Africans, it's said, *sex* is what you carry coal in, while *six* is needed for procreation! So what happens to *pit* in these circumstances? That vowel becomes more central (more like *the*). Rawbone Malong wrote the South African equivalent to *Let Stalk Strine*: he called it *Ah Big Yaws* (*I Beg Yours*; i.e. pardon), and you can see that vowel quality in some of his 'translations' from Standard English. Look at what happens to *it* when 'Would you mind passing it to me?' becomes 'Chuck a tear'.

- The puff of air that follows the articulation of the voiceless consonants at the beginning of words like *pit*, *tip*, and *cot* in RP is called aspiration. (You can feel it if you hold the back of your hand up to your mouth while saying these words. The effect isn't there when you say the voiced sounds *bit*, *dip*, or *got*). This doesn't usually happen in South African English, which is why outsiders sometimes mishear *pat* as *bat*, and so on.

- The most distinctive feature of the accent lies in its rhythm, which is much more staccato than in RP. The British accent has a 'tum-te-tum' rhythmical character – as heard in most of Shakespeare, for example ('To be or not to be . . .') – with the stressed syllables separated by unstressed syllables. South African English has a 'rat-a-tat-a-tat' character, with each syllable carrying a stronger degree of stress. The same kind of effect (linguists call it 'syllable-timed' rhythm) can also be heard in Indian English and Caribbean English.

PART THREE

ACCENTS PAST

WHERE IT ALL BEGAN

DAVID   There have always been accents. There was never a time when just one accent was used by everyone who spoke English. We can deduce this from the way the language first arrived in Britain. After the Romans left the British Isles, the Britons living in what is now England were attacked by tribes from the north (the Picts and Scots), and appealed for help from the Saxon peoples living in the north of mainland Europe. The first ships arrived in AD 449, and others followed, landing in different parts of the south and east coasts.

The historian Bede tells us that the new arrivals were from 'the three most powerful nations of Germany – Saxons, Angles, and Jutes'. He goes on to suggest that the Jutes settled in Kent and the Isle of Wight, the Saxons across the southern counties, and the Angles in the east, midlands, and north. We have to take his descriptions with a large pinch of salt, for we know very little about the tribes he names, and he was in any case writing some 300 years later. But it's clear that the Anglo-Saxons, as they came to be called – a name that distinguished them from the continental Saxons – were a diverse lot, who must have spoken different dialects. And when their language was first written down, starting in the seventh century, we see signs of the different accents reflected in the spellings used by the scribes.

Only around 3,000 manuscripts survive from those early days, in the period from 600 to 1150, known as Old English – around three million words. That seems like a lot until we reflect that this is less than a single modern author might write. Charles Dickens, for instance, penned over four million. But four main dialects emerge out of the Anglo-Saxon darkness: Kentish, in the south-east; West Saxon, across the south, in such areas as modern Hampshire and Sussex; Mercian, across the Midlands; and Northumbrian, in the north-east. There would have been other dialects too, but the texts we have reflect the locations of the monasteries where the scribes were writing.

There was no standard spelling in those days, so the scribes used whatever letters they felt best represented the sounds they heard, and did this in a very systematic way. The word for a 'stone' was spelled *ston* in the south and *stan* in the north. We can still hear it pronounced that way in Scotland, in Northern Ireland, and parts of north-east England. The Irish folk-singer Johnny McEvoy has it in the title of his Scottish epic, 'The Wee Magic Stane'. And 'A rolling stone gathers no moss' is, in Scots, 'A rowin stane gaithers nae fug'.

We can see three accents in the surviving manuscripts of the Lord's Prayer. In a West Saxon version the first line appears like this:

fæder ure þu þe eart on heofonum

(literally: father our, you who art in heaven).
In a Mercian text, it is like this:

feder ure þu eart in heofenum

and in a Northumbrian text, it is like this:

fader urer ðu art in heofnum.

We can work out from the spellings that the vowel of 'father' in Northumbria was made with the tongue low down and central in the mouth, similar to what we hear when people from the north of England today say a word like *cap*. In Mercia, it was higher up and further forward, more like the vowel in *set*, as pronounced in present-day RP. And in West Saxon, it was somewhere in between – more like the vowel of *man* in RP.

THE SHAKESPEARE SOUND

BEN   The room is dark, candles littered around the space. The actors I've been working with for the last few weeks are nervous, but excited. We're about to do something that so many actors strive for, but few attain: something brand new with Shakespeare. We're about to recite one of Shakespeare's plays in the reconstructed accent that he and his company of fellow Elizabethan actors would actually have spoken in.

After rehearsal the night before, we had retired to the tavern across the road to divvy up the spear-carrier parts of *The Tragedy of Pericles, Prince of Tyre*. Each actor had learned his or her own lines, and the cues of when to speak, but we'd only rehearsed the dances and the fights en masse, and no traditional rehearsal or run-through of the scenes had taken place. The first time we would speak our lines to each other would be in front of our waiting, candlelit audience, and so it would also be the first time that we as a Company would hear the play as a whole. And the first time anyone has heard this play in OP – Original Pronunciation – for 400 years.

Hilton, playing Gower, shuffles into the centre of the stage. He opens his mouth, and begins to speak:

> To sing a song that old was sung,
> From ashes ancient Gower is come.

In OP, the word *Gower* is pronounced 'Gohrrr' – and the sound sends a bolt of electricity around the room, striking back at the stage beneath our feet and sizzling Shakespeare's chorus into life like Shelley's monster, while Hilton begins to move about the stage with a physicality like nothing I've ever seen before . . .

When Dad first started exploring 'OP' in workshops at Shakespeare's Globe in 2004, I didn't, to my shame, pay much attention.* But family rivalry aside, it's also fair to say that, in hearing about Dad's work, I had fundamentally misunderstood the point of OP. As I said earlier, I'd sometimes used my home-town accent when privately rehearsing audition speeches for productions of Shakespeare, but I'd never used it in the audition itself, let alone the growling, earthier tones of OP.

Said aloud, would Shakespeare's accent even be under-

---

* All right, I admit that I was in a bit of a huff because I couldn't take part in the work myself, because
a) I had auditioned for the production and didn't get a part (worse: I gave a terrible, head-shaking, embarrassing audition, and I think the director said something like I wasn't 'his type of actor')
b) by 2004 I would have happily swept the stage at the Globe, so entranced by the place I was, and
c) this technically meant my father had beaten me to working there, darn him.

stood nowadays? Or would it sound like your English Literature teacher trying to read out Chaucer? Secondly, I have to admit that I couldn't yet see the dramaturgical use, either. Yes, it's interesting to see actors in 'original practice' costumes, doublet-and-hosed up to the neck, but it doesn't necessarily make Shakespeare any more accessible to young minds, addled from years of having to read plays out loud behind desks in a classroom.

And then, one day, I read a line in one of Dad's books about the Globe exploration into how Shakespeare himself might have spoken: "The lack of an upper-class accent is the single biggest barrier to thinking ourselves into the auditory mindset of the Elizabethans.'

What Dad was saying is that, as far as we can tell, there was no 'upper-class accent' in Shakespeare's time – and that means that back then, if you wanted to act like a king or a commoner, you couldn't simply use an accent to demonstrate your social standing. 'So how do we show who's King or who's not?', asked an actor.

'Act,' said the director.

This caught my attention. One day soon after that, Dad came back from a rehearsal at the Globe.

D – The Master of Movement† was in today.

---

* For those interested, the book is called *Think On My Words: Exploring Shakespeare's Language* (Cambridge University Press, 2008).

† In the first ten years of the reconstructed Globe's life, the specialist advisers in charge of helping actors with their text, voice, or movement, were given Elizabethan-style titles, so the Master of Movement, Master of Text, Master of Voice. The 'Master of Movement' (Glynn Macdonald)

– Oh yeah?

D – Yes – you'll like this – she leant over as they were doing a run-through of the play, and whispered, 'My goodness, the actors are *moving* differently.'

My ears pricked up. This idea – that speaking Shakespeare in the accent that the plays were originally written for might provoke a different *movement* dynamic in actors – made sense with an almost audible click. Ever since then I have been on a different path with Shakespeare.

Having initially hated him at school, as I grew older I discovered a joy in his works in their natural context – acting them, in other words. I spent years taking workshops with physical theatre companies, learning a new movement craft and trying to find ways to combine great verse-speaking with great movement, to move away from the stand-stock-still-and-declaim style of performing Shakespeare. And yet, even as I grew closer to his work, I had a sense that *something* was missing. I perhaps hadn't been able to articulate it at the time, but speaking Shakespeare in RP, much like the idea of a doublet and hose, had always felt unnecessarily restrictive to me. Dad's work suddenly made the plays feel relevant in a way they never had before.

It was beautiful, actually. Dad has always said he lives his acting life through me by proxy (which is how I first learnt the word), and the frustrated actor inside of him was sated as the cast dragged him – literally – onto the stage in front of a

---

looked after the way the actors moved about the stage and used their bodies.

full cheering house at the last OP performance. My dad, the Master of Pronunciation at Shakespeare's Globe. That is a pride-maker.

We have a pretty good idea of how OP sounds, but I'll leave it to Dad to play Sherlock Holmes to my—

D – Watson?

. . . *Moriarty*, with the linguistic clues. The thing that bakes my biscuit is how it feels to dust these old words down, and speak them to an audience.

Original Pronunciation, with its vowels further back and lower in the mouth, activates the lower register in your voice (a much more useful vocal range for, say, projecting it into a circular outdoor Globe-like theatre space). This shifts your acting centre (the focal point of your energy) from up in the throat to down into your gut and groin. In turn, this makes actors earthier and rougher in their delivery, an ocean's leap away from the careful, stiffly delivered stance that RP so often generates.

Combine all *that* with Hamlet's recommendation to 'Speak the speech I pray you, as I pronounce it to you, trippingly on the tongue, but do not mouth it as many of our players do . . .' * and you have actors, boy and girl, making heartfelt, earthy, practical choices with their interpretations, being clearly heard despite speaking fast†, and

---

* Where *trippingly* means with alacrity, and *do not mouth* basically means don't overdo it.

† It's a common misunderstanding that poetry makes more sense when you slow down. If you listen to the UK poet Simon Armitage or

most of all, moving around the stage with drive and purpose. Hamlet becomes the action hero, rather than the indecisive, passive over-thinker:

Tuh be ohr nat tuh be, that is the kwestyun . . .

A lower centre of gravity, a deeper voice, more natural colour,* the subsequent honest interpretation of the lines – and because you're moving differently, sounding differently, and vocalizing differently, the words feel new and sparkle in the air. They feel crumbly and chewy in your mouth, like listening to a kindly old train conductor. You begin to understand the characters' words as human speech rather than as lines of poetry . . .

. . . which is the point where I hand over the metaphorical reins of this physiological linguistic phenomenon to my father, who will hopefully explain just *why* this happens, before I wade too far out of my acting shallows into the darker, murkier waters of Dad's pools.

DAVID It's well worthwhile trying to record accents before they disappear. That's what made the BBC *Voices* project of 2005 so appealing. It was the first nationwide attempt to take, as it were, an 'auditory snapshot' of accents and dialects in the UK. In fifty years, it will be an invaluable

---

Poet Laureate Carol Ann Duffy read their own work in their northern accents, the *last* thing they do is read leisurely.

* *War* sounds like *wahrrrrrr*, something full of sound and fury, rather than a polite disagreement over tea.

record of the way people spoke at the beginning of the century.

If only we had such a record from times past – from the 1940s, say, or the 1930s. The few radio recordings we have from those decades are only the tiniest tip of the accent iceberg. We shall never know how the mass of ordinary people spoke across the whole country in the 1930s. But even fragments of audio recordings from earlier times are better than nothing.

How far back can we listen? In theory, 1877, when Thomas Alvar Edison invented a means of recording sound. But not much has survived. One of the earliest examples is a phonographic cylinder recorded on 30 July 1890. On it you can hear the voice of Florence Nightingale.

In May of that year it was reported in the press that many veterans of the Charge of the Light Brigade in the Crimean War were living in appalling poverty. Despite public outrage, the government failed to act, so the St James's Gazette set up the Light Brigade Relief Fund. Edison's representative in Britain arranged for three recordings to be made to support the fund. One was of a veteran trumpeter sounding the charge as heard at Balaclava. Another was of Lord Tennyson reading his poem about the event. And the third was a message from Miss Nightingale to the veterans, recorded at her home at 10 South Street, off Park Lane in London.

We hear her saying her name and the date, and then, 'When I am no longer even a memory, just a name, I hope my voice may perpetuate the great work of my life. God bless my dear old comrades of Balaclava and bring them safe to shore.

Florence Nightingale.' Her accent is reminiscent of the voices heard in early BBC recordings of the 1920s. She says *thirtieth* with the first vowel close to the one in modern *car*. *Ninety* ends with a short open vowel, rhyming more with modern *say* than *see*. If only there were more of it recorded. The fragment we have of this century-old accent is tantalizing.

And that's it. To find out how people spoke before the 1870s we have to rely on other sources of evidence and our own powers of deduction as accentologists. Sherlock again.

The sources

The big dictionaries written since the eighteenth century can tell us a lot, as the editors would include a pronunciation for each of the words. It would be a personal view, of course, and the focus would be on just one accent, but this would usually be enough to identify earlier pronunciations of words that have since changed their sound. We find them describing the pronunciation of *oblige* as *obleege*, *daughters* as *darters*, and *china* as *chayney*, and showing how the stress pattern of certain words was different from what it is today, as in *balCOny* and *comPENsate*. We can even sometimes date the change: dictionaries published before 1800 show *balcony* with the older stress pattern only; those after the 1850s show the new pattern only.

What the dictionaries say is sometimes reinforced by anecdotes. Additional evidence comes from the complaints people made about changes in pronunciation. In *Recollections of the Table-talk of Samuel Rogers,* published just after his death in 1855, we read:

> The now fashionable pronunciation of several words is to me at least very offensive: *CONtemplate* – is bad enough; but *BALcony* makes me sick.

Before the era of big dictionaries, a surprising number of people wrote books or essays on pronunciation. Fascination with English accents isn't solely a modern phenomenon. Variation and change intrigued observers in the sixteenth and seventeenth centuries too, especially if they were interested in how poetry was to be performed or if they were involved in proposals to reform English spelling. And the writers often give us very precise and detailed clues as to how words were pronounced in their day.

As an example, listen to this famous couplet from one of Shakespeare's best-known sonnets – number 116, sometimes called the 'marriage' sonnet, because couples often ask for it to be read out on their wedding day. It begins, 'Let me not to the marriage of true minds / Admit impediments . . .' and ends:

> If this be error and upon me proved,
> I never writ, nor no man ever loved.

A sonnet is supposed to rhyme, and here we have a couplet which doesn't. What's going on?

The pronunciation has changed since 1600, that's all. But which way? Did *love* rhyme with *prove* – 'loove', as it were? Or did *prove* rhyme with *love*? It was the latter. How do we know? Because writers of the time tell us so. Ben Jonson, the playwright, also wrote an English grammar, and in the introduction to that work he goes through the letters of the alphabet and tells us how they are pronounced. When he gets to letter *O*, we read, 'In the short time more flat, and akin to *u*; as . . . *brother, love, prove*'.

If we read through all the people who wrote about pronunciation in a particular period, we can piece together quite a good picture of the accents that were around at the time. The writers don't always agree, of course – any more than they do today. Which is the modern pronunciation of *again* – rhyming with *main* or with *men*? Do you pronounce the *t* in *often*? Is it 'shedule' or 'skedule'? But there's agreement about most of the words in use today, and we see a similar agreement in earlier periods – certainly enough to reconstruct a plausible 'original pronunciation' of the time.

The deductions

But observers never observe everything. And sometimes we can't trust what they say. Imagine reading a book today which tells us that there is only one way to pronounce the word *controversy*, and that's with the stress on the first syllable: *CONtroversy*. We wouldn't credit the writer's opinion, because we all know that there's another pronunciation with the stress on the second syllable: *conTROVersy*. Such writers do exist, presenting their own usage as if it were the only one, and insisting that everyone else should speak as they do. They existed in earlier times too.

Today, to find evidence of the alternatives that occur we only have to listen. In earlier periods, we have to be more of an accent detective. Let's continue with Shakespeare. As the *loved/proved* example suggests, one of the big sources of evidence is going to be the rhymes that he and his contemporaries used. Linguists have worked their way through all the rhymes that they can find, and identified various trends. They've found, for example, that the vowel in *doom* sounded like the one in *come*, and that the vowel in *wars* sounded like the one in *stars*. And after going through all the vowels and consonants in this way, it's possible to construct an outline of a Shakespearean accent.

But what about words that don't turn up in any rhymes? Now linguists have to do a different kind of survey, looking at spellings. The English spelling system took a thousand years to evolve, and at any time it provides us with information about how words were pronounced. We know, for instance, that some accents in Shakespeare's day pronounced *murder* as *murther*, as the word is often spelled with a *th*. *Film* in *Romeo and Juliet* is spelled *philome*, suggesting that it had two syllables – much as we hear in modern Irish accents today, 'fillum'. Spellings provide us with a great deal of additional information.

And there's yet another source of evidence – cases where a piece of wordplay works only if a particular pronunciation is assumed. Take the name *Ajax*. The Elizabethan courtier and writer John Harington, unable to stand the stench, proposed a lavatory with a flushing mechanism. Smells, it was believed, carried infections. In 1596 he presented his ideas in *A New Discourse upon a Stale Subject: the Metamorphosis of Ajax. Ajax* was a pun on 'a jakes', which is how the name was pronounced at the time. As a result, Ajax quickly became yet another name for a lavatory. It's still used in that way in some regional dialects: one goes 'to the jakes'.

In Shakespeare's *Troilus and Cressida*, there's a lumpish Greek soldier called Ajax, who is something of a butt to his companions. In one scene, he and Thersites – one of the characters often found hanging around an army camp in those days – trade insults. Thersites howls at the others, 'But yet you look not well upon him; for whosoever you take him to be, he is Ajax'. To the modern listener and reader, this is a puzzle. Why should the simple saying of his name be an insult? But if we remember the Elizabethan pronunciation, we see that Thersites was being as rude as he could, calling him, in effect, a shithouse.

Shakespeare also shows us that *jakes* was definitely a risqué word at the time. Why else would Touchstone the jester be worried about it? In *As You Like It*, he meets Jaques, the philosopher-courtier, in the forest. The name Jaques would also have been pronounced 'jakes', and this is enough to make Touchstone feel awkward – or perhaps he is being deliberately provocative – for he refers to Jaques as 'Master What-ye-call't'.

It wasn't just Touchstone who was sensitive. John Harington has the following anecdote at the very beginning of his book (I've modernized his spelling and punctuation):

There was a very tall and serviceable gentleman, some-time Lieutenant of the ordinance, called M. Jaques Wingfield, who coming one day, either of business or of kindness, to visit a great Lady in the Court, the Lady bade her gentlewoman ask which of the Wingfields it was. He told her Jaques Wingfield. The modest gentlewoman, that was not so well seen [familiar] in the French to know that Jaques was but James in English, was so bashful that to mend the matter (as she thought) she brought her Lady word, not without blushing, that it was M. Privy Wingfield; at which I suppose the Lady then – I am sure the Gentleman after, as long as he lived – was wont to make great sport.

Playing with the name *Jaques* must have been a standing joke in the England of Queen Elizabeth.

Early accents

Using evidence of the kind I've just described, we can work out the sound system of the period when Shakespeare was writing – Early Modern English. And using similar techniques, we can reconstruct earlier systems of English pronunciation, going right back to Old English. We'll never be able to work out all the accent variations there would have been. There's always an element of guesswork. But we can find out enough to capture their overall character.

For instance, one of the most noticeable features of

English spoken around the year 1600 was the way words ending in such spellings as –*tion* and –*cian* – *invention, salvation, musician* and so on – were pronounced with the individual consonants and vowels separate. 'In-ven-see-on.' 'Sal-vay-see-on.' 'Mu-zi-see-an.' When a sequence of such words appears, the distinctive character of the old accent soon builds up. No modern accent displays such a feature.

The best way to experience the results of this reconstruction is to see a production from one of the companies that have put on a play in Original Pronunciation – or OP, as it's usually called. Shakespeare's Globe in London was the initiator of the current interest in this approach. Sam Wanamaker's inspired reconstruction of the Globe theatre in 1997 led to a renewed interest in 'original practices' – such as original costumes, music, instruments, and movement – and it was only natural that in due course the company would experiment with the pronunciation. An OP production of *Romeo and Juliet* took place in the Globe's 2004 season. And over the next decade, several other productions followed, in both Britain and the USA.

Nor is it only Shakespeare who has been the focus of interest. OP has been used to read texts of other poets, playwrights, and prose writers of the period (such as John Donne). The 400th anniversary of the King James Bible in 2011 motivated several readings in OP, as did the British Library's 2010–11 exhibition, *Evolving English*. And people interested in early music have experimented with OP, as have those involved in heritage tourism (to Jacobethan-period locations). In fact, it's in the early music arena that you're most likely to have heard snatches of OP before. Or in an Anglican church where they sing 'And grant us thy sal-vay-see-on'.

OP performance brings us as close as possible to how old texts would have sounded. It enables us to hear effects lost when old texts are read in a modern way. And it avoids the modern social connotations that arise when we hear old texts read in a present-day accent. New assonances and rhythms give lines a fresh impact. It suggests fresh contrasts in speech style, such as between young and old, court and commoners, or literate and illiterate; and it motivates unexpected possibilities of character interpretation.

What reconstructions can't do is tell us much about the accent of an individual. For that we need contemporary accounts, and just occasionally we get a hint. Scots King James I is described by Francis Bacon as speaking 'in the full dialect of his country'. And we know that Sir Walter Raleigh spoke Early Modern English with a Devonshire accent. The seventeenth-century biographer John Aubrey was told by an old man who had known Raleigh that he 'spake broad Devonshire to his dying day'. And Queen Elizabeth gave him the nickname 'Water', reflecting the way Raleigh would drop his *l*s. But nobody ever bothered to tell us how Shakespeare himself spoke. That's a shame.

THE SHIBBOLETH OF STAUNTON

BEN

Jeremy – *Alright, mate?* Nobody says that. You say that over here, and someone will reply, *Do I look like something's wrong? Cheers* isn't something we say here either, with the softer *r*. And there are certain questions, *You takin' the piss?* with that particular lilt. We say, *Are you taking the piss?* It's never rhetorical.

– Is that true for everyone in Staunton, do you think?

J – It's pronounced *Stan-tun*.

– But it's spelt *Staunton*.

J – Yeah.

– So it's like Shrewsbury is pronounced *Shrows-berry*?

J – Where?

– It doesn't matter.

J – Well, if you pronounce it *Staun-tun*, we know you're not from here, that's all.

I was sitting on a porch in Staunton, Virginia, talking with an actor from the Blackfriars Theatre – a recreation of the indoor theatre that Shakespeare's Company moved to from the outdoor Globe, around 1607. If you ever go to see one of the late plays, like *The Tempest, The Winter's Tale,* or *Coriolanus,* for all their scale in terms of the exploration of the human condition, they were written for a small, intimate theatre, performed out of the reach of natural daylight. To light the stage they used candles that smoked a lot and burned quickly, meaning the chandeliers would need to be lowered and raised between acts, one reason we now have intervals as part of theatre etiquette.*

The Blackfriars Theatre had asked me to come and give a talk on Original Pronunciation, and over the previous month I'd covered three-quarters of the United States giving similar introductions to this new-old aesthetic.

When I was invited to give the talk I was simply told that it garnered genuine fascination: a desire to hear Shakespeare spoken in anything other than Received Pronunciation or Good American. The reason I had arrived at before my trip had begun was that it brought *ownership,* and I'd experienced similar reactions a couple of years earlier as Artist in Residence in Reno, Nevada, leading a half-student, half-semi-professional company in the contemporary world premiere of *Hamlet* in OP.

Ownership of Shakespeare is a tricky beast to describe. In the UK we're saddled with Shakespeare as part of our heritage, so ownership is inherent. In other countries, Shakespeare is adored, but ownership feels restricted because no one feels

---

* Most theatres now insist on having a break because there's money to be made on interval drinks. Most actors and audiences insist on interval drinks, full stop.

they have the 'right' accent. Certainly, non-RP Shakespeare in the UK is a rarity. There's a theatre company in the north of England called Northern Broadsides that only uses regional accents in their Shakespeare productions. The bigger companies in the UK, though, tend more towards regional accents only for the comedic characters; the nobles invariably speak RP, and have done so since before Laurence Olivier in the forties, and pretty much ever since the actor David Garrick's renaissance of Shakespeare in the late eighteenth century.

This performance practice was passed down into the repertory theatre system of the mid-to-late twentieth century, where actors learnt how to act by *acting*, * becoming members of companies that would stage a new production every week, and you would graduate from spear carrier to messenger to Lord to best friend, then to clown or lead, villain or hero, old man or nurse, depending on your personal area of expertise.

This is how it had been since Shakespeare's time. Nowadays, unless you're really lucky, instead of learning by doing, you go to drama school, and learn by practise and getting it wrong with a non-paying, pedagogical audience watching and critiquing you.

Part of that received pedagogy is to speak Shakespeare in Received Pronunciation, and to shift your regional accent to home / friend use only. Combine that with Garrick's efforts

---

* As opposed to by theory, in drama school. The repertory system of theatre, killed off by the cuts in the late 1970s/early 1980s, gave us a terrific heritage of actors. See page 191.

to re-engage the British public with this Elizabethan play-wright by re-introducing him as Master Poet, and Shakespeare has (over the last 150 years) been turned back into the Immortal Bard, Radio 4's Man of the Millennium, the plague of exam-hall imprisoned teenagers, and the theatrical equiv-alent of an international chequebook as the entire world comes on board with this man's unique ability to see so completely into the human soul.

I say *back into*, because the sobriquet 'Immortal Bard' was coined by his contemporaries on the title page of a collection of his plays back in 1623. He went out of fashion, as every-thing else did in the seventeenth century. The Puritans took over, the monarchy fell; Christmas was cancelled; theatre, and fun in general was vetoed. So when the monarchy returned in 1660, everyone was so grumpy from Being Serious All The Time that when Shakespeare was staged, the endings had been rewritten, turning tragedy into rom-com (Romeo and Juliet survive!).

So Shakespeare arrived in the twentieth century, resplen-dent in his new-found new-old glory, raised back onto a dais, the books in the library quietly moved from the Theatre section to the Literature floor. And at exactly the same time, Received Pronunciation was rapidly segregating Britain's social classes and making work for the likes of Henry Higgins.

This distinction didn't exist in Shakespeare's time. It wasn't possible to perceive someone's economic or cultural background from their voice. You could tell what part of the country someone was from, and you could probably hear whether someone was educated or not (if they pronounced their *h* they had learned to read, and had seen there was an *h* in the spelling; if they hadn't learned to read, they wouldn't have seen how it was spelled, so wouldn't know to sound the letter out).

Received Pronunciation changed all that, and gave the elite the chance to demonstrate their wealth, health, and knowledge simply from the way they made noises in their mouth. It was the ultimate invisible membership badge.

Shakespeare, now considered to be the greatest poet, (and, latterly, playwright) was pushed to the top of the canon of English Literature. When spoken, it was to be spoken as carefully and clearly as possible. These were not humans speaking dialogue that just happened to use poetry to express themselves (as characters in musicals burst into song because there's no other way to convey the emotions they're feeling): the characters were devices to write the highest calibre of poetry.

The only accent that could achieve this level of clarity and care was considered to be RP, because it was associated with all that was great, good, wise, rich, scholarly, and intellectual.

Shakespeare became beautiful. Not because he gets his characters to come on stage and rip out their hearts, thrusting a mirror into his audiences' faces and demanding of them if they have ever known what love is, if they've ever felt jealousy, if they've ever been disloyal, if they've ever killed. Beautiful because it now *sounded* beautiful, rendered in the accent of the stiff upper lip, of Noël Coward's decorum, and certainly not anyone who might wear their heart on their sleeve.

Flash forward fifty years, and the sound associated with good Shakespeare is *only* RP, while regional accents have established themselves in British minds as either comforting (Yorkshire), rough (Cockney), cheeky (Manchester, Liverpool), unintelligible (Geordie, Glasgow), dozy (Somerset, Cornwall, and Devon), or stupid (Birmingham) – to name just a few.

None of this was true, but the accent-sounds had gained stereotypes indelibly written into their very essence, creating such strong impressions that, as we've seen, your intelligence and education (or lack thereof) was judged on what part of the country you were from, irrespective of whether you were a brain surgeon or a road-sweeper, just because you opened your mouth and uttered words.

Interviewees would dull, smother, flatten or drown out the accent of their home, to avoid raising any eyebrows. RP was as important as being able to type, especially if you answered the phone . . .

Regional accents were reserved for characters like the comedic rustics in *A Midsummer Night's Dream*. Half your work was done. Speak the lines in a Birmingham accent, and job done: no acting required.

On the flip side, you don't need to *act* noble, you only need to *sound* like you're part of the upper classes. Someone wrote in the *Evening Standard* in 2014,

A less deferential society requires a tricky combination of

fluency and classlessness. It is why urbane Scots like Andrew Neil and Michael Gove thrive in public life, being both eloquent yet not grating. (Don't all tweet at once.)

David Cameron is a fluent speaker, but those patrician vowels grate. Boris Johnson masks his 'yah-yah' delivery with broad comedy. Tony Blair introduced a glottal stop and 'y'knows' which they most definitely did not teach him at Fettes.

At Oxford, a talented friend who wanted to act was distraught not to get the part of Alice in Wonderland on the amazingly stupid grounds that her accent was too northern for a child of the shires. Nowadays, there is barely a Cordelia on stage who is not invested with a broad regional lilt (the National favours the North-West).

That's not to say that in the 1970s there weren't mind-blowing, staggering, heartbreaking performances given by actors speaking RP – this was the period that saw all the current Hollywood arch-villains and wise-mentors begin to spread their theatrical wings: Michael Gambon, Patrick Stewart, Ian McKellen, Maggie Smith, Judi Dench, Anthony Hopkins, Helen Mirren, Ian Holm (or Dumbledore, Professor Xavier, Magneto / Gandalf, Minerva McGonagall, M, Hannibal, The Queen, and Frodo) and many others were frequently setting the benchmark higher and higher in English theatre, never once (or very, very rarely) using the accents they grew up with.

So if the accent you're using is doing a lot of the storytelling for you, immediately instilling in your audience's minds a sort of character-CV, a life history as immediately telling as whether they're wearing jeans or a suit on a Monday morning in the 1980s, it's easy to see how two things happen:

One, if you want to do any of the great Shakespearean lead characters 'properly', you need to speak in this beautiful, musical accent. So if you're American, you're stuffed.

Two, if you can naturally speak in RP, acting becomes only about putting on a voice, and you become lazy, letting the accent do all the work.

Both result in pushing the audience away. The performances are thin, and almost impossible to relate to. And because characters stop being human and are only amalgamations of musical sounds, the link to opera was already being forged. Around the mid-twentieth century, Shakespeare's big speeches (like King Lear's Act 2, Scene 4, *O reason not the need . . .*) stopped being thought of as speeches and started being referred to as *arias,* that you literally almost sing, such is the focus on the sound quality and rhythm.

Watching Shakespeare became diffused, as characters would talk about being utterly heartbroken but actually only look very, very slightly discomfited, perhaps with one single tear: the accent was creating a barrier in the audience between those who were part of the culture that used the accent and those that weren't. And those ones that weren't were often under the impression they were being mocked.

Speaking Shakespeare became a private club, and if you were from South Africa, Australia, America, India, France, Holland, Ireland, Scotland (or anywhere other than from wherever RP comes) and tried to speak Shakespeare, you were, right off the bat, inferior in quality, irrespective of how good an actor you were.

Original Pronunciation, built from the many accents that sailed away from England, the ancestors of all these English-speaking colonies carrying with them their copies of Shakespeare's plays along with their Bibles, bestows owner-ship of Shakespeare on their descendants. As Shakespeare tried to hold a mirror up to our lives, Original Pronunciation echoes vowel qualities of the accent you, as a twenty-first century speaker of English, talk in every day.

As the accent of Shakespeare's Britain travelled around the world, depending on which shore you landed on, differ-ent flecks of it continued while others were lost. It means that an American and a Brit and an Australian living in 2014, coming together to speak in Original Pronunciation, would each discover that some vowels are more natural to them because they are already part of their daily speech, while others are completely alien and need to be rediscovered.

In Shakespeare's time, English was described by William Camden[*] as a language that 'some spoke broadly, some flatly and not a few mincingly'. But while we have little clues else about the musicality – the tone and pitch – we can be pretty accurate about the rest. It's an accent that was jeered at, that was often heckled, and had to be heard over a generally raucous crowd. RP is an accent designed to be listened to in

---

[*] 1551–1623. English historian, antiquarian, topographer, and Clar-enceux King of Arms. Greatest job title ever.

quiet rooms, bristling with modern conventions of theatre etiquette: sit in the dark and listen quietly, rather than stand outside in the (relatively) fresh sunny air and drink beer. RP has little place at the football pitch, and going to the Globe in 1600 would have been like a trip to the Superbowl.

So if there's a problem with attempts to make modern Shakespeare performance accessible, it's because it has nothing to do with setting it in a world of mobile phones, it's (in part) because we're speaking it in an accent it simply wasn't designed for. As Dad said, rhymes falter, and as far as I'm concerned that drags us out of the world of the play; jokes fail to make us laugh; and when audience members with regional accents hear the accent of Olivier and Gielgud, their brain tells them it has the identity marker of 'posh', and switch off – hearing a society club they don't have access to, and are not invited to join; a performance that is to be listened to, certainly, and perhaps only secondarily to be engaged with.

It makes a certain sense that the RP accent has been used over the last century for Shakespeare: it's a heightened accent, with a crisp, melodic clarity to it, and so theoretically it would make the elevated verse-speech Shakespeare often wrote in sound even more heightened, more beautiful, grander.

But when OP was spoken for the first time in 2004 at the Globe, kids in the audience said, 'They sound like us.' What they meant was, the characters didn't sound like 'them'. The accent gave them ownership through recognition of a sound they intuitively knew like the back of their hand.

When they said, 'They sound like us,' they didn't mean it in a literal sense. OP doesn't – can't – sound like every regional accent, of course. And yet by some strange magic, it sort of does. It has flecks of Irish, Somerset, Norfolk, Scots, Cockney and many others. It has Australian in a word like *yet* (*yit*) and Canadian in a word like *house (howce)* or *about (aboot)*. So there is a natural element to it that echoes *you*.

And perhaps that isn't so surprising. Elizabethan London was a melting pot of accents, the beating heart of a great sovereign nation. People came from all over the country, their accents fused together, and as we saw earlier, later on they went to southern ports, and the accent travelled the Atlantic. Later still the accent got sent to Bristol, and sailed down to the Antipodes. So when I ask people (particularly young-lings) what accents OP reminds them of, they often call out every English accent from Dublin to *Pirates of the Caribbean*.

What seems to happen to audiences is this: they listen to Shakespeare in RP; it is the sound of poetry, of literature, of old memories of study and exam, so they listen with their heads. When they listen to Shakespeare in OP, it is the sound of earth, of emotion, a new-old sound that has shimmers of the accent they grew up speaking, and so they listen with their hearts, making them perk up just as the smell of a famil-iar childhood meal would.

Speaking in OP was easier than I thought it might be because of my transatlantic friends and travels, I already had a relatively hard *r* in my accent, similar to Somerset or the pirate accent. *Sarrvice, hee-yerrrr*, for 'Service, here'. The Canadian 'out', that features in OP, I struggled much harder with. The American cast members of the OP *Hamlet* had all naturally grown up fondly satirising their neighbours across their northern border, and so found 'out' easier to sound. The Australian yet (*yit*) my American colleagues struggled more with, while I had no problem – ten years of watching our colonial *Neighbours* and *Home and Away* while teenagering finally proving of use.

Having said that, I spent three months in Reno ('The Biggest Li'l City In The World'), and I never managed a Nevada accent. I was lambasted for recording the voice-over for the TV commercial spot advertising our show. When I came to the company name, I had to say, 'Performed by the Nevahhda Repertory Company.'

I returned to rehearsal, and twenty voices, as one, shouted, 'It's not *Nevahhda*, it's *Nevada!*'

Still, I found myself forever slipping into a stronger and stronger American accent outside of rehearsal. As an Austrian actor-friend put it to me while I was writing this book, having noticed his accent shift and change as he works around the world, he unwittingly described the linguistic phenomenon of *accommodation*: 'I take the accent from the people that I'm living with.'

It was tempting to imagine a *Love, Actually* situation while I was in Reno, not as Hugh Grant the Prime Minister, but the Kris Marshall character storyline, arriving in America and immediately being beset with people dropping at my feet at the first syllable of my British accent. 'Having an accent' is thought to be the key that unlocks the door to free drinks and hearts.

This, I hasten to add, didn't ever happen. Although the only time I ever actively used my British accent for personal gain was, well, when I got pulled over by a cop for going (slightly) too fast.

Cop – Sir, did you know you were going 60 in a 50 zone?

– Oh gosh, was I? I'm frightfully sorry, officer; it's all this mile-per-hour, kilometres-per-hour business; I'm still getting used to it. I'm terribly, terribly sorry. I thought I *was* doing 50.

Cop – . . . OK. Well, you go easy now, and thank you.

Did he just thank me? Did I just turn into Hugh Grant? Shut up, indicate, pull away slowly. I glanced in the rear-view mirror. If I tried to wheedle my way out of an awkward situation like that in the UK, if anything, I'd roughen the edges of my accent and sound less privileged.

I looked back at the dials in front of me. Hm. I learned to drive in miles per hour, just like the American mileometer on the other side of my steering wheel. Apparently, the cop didn't know that *Europe* has kilometres per hour, and that measurement is as alien to me as it is to an American. RP as a protest-of-innocence, a get-out-of-jail-free card in the US.

Who knew? Perhaps RP isn't as villainous as I thought.

PART FOUR

ACCENTS FUTURE

WHAT WENT WRONG IN BETELGEUSE?

BEN Nowadays, a person's accent is often the last thing you learn about them. You don't hear someone's voice until *after* stalking their Facebook page, looking through their links on a Twitter feed, their Tumblr posts, and judging their artistic merits as a photographer by the types of subjects and styles of shots on their Instagram profile.

Possibly, *maybe* after processing all these expressions of self, you *might* hear their accent. There is (as of 2014) no mass convention or expectation of a vocal introduction to a personal area of the Web, the equivalent of an answer-machine message welcoming a visitor to one of the representations of your virtual self. The online world, vlogs and podcasts aside, is relatively quiet. The people I tweet with, for the most part, I have never met, and my ears have never heard their accent.

So are we heading towards a future without accents? When I think of the accents of the future, I hear an alien, and a robot.

Nanu-nanu, Danger, Will Robinson, DANGER!

If, like me, you were alive and watching TV in the latter

half of the twentieth century, you might recall the late Robin Williams' alien Mork in the US TV show *Mork and Mindy* as a kind of crazed, stilted, utterly antisocial, wacky, overly sensitive alien in a human form. If he greeted someone in his alien language, he would say, '*Nanu-nanu*,' in a slightly staccato manner, but everything else was clearly a Chicago-born, Californian-living accent.

Robots are man-made, designed ever-closer to human form, but rarely *sounding* human. They more often involve a whirring, clanking speech like the Robot in the TV show *Lost in Space* (1965–1968), and are definitely deep-voiced in tone. *I, Robot* in 2004 was a decent example to the contrary with Sonny's boy-male flutey tones, or the boy-Robot in Spielberg's *AI* from 2001. Kubrick (who had the idea for *AI*) brought us Arthur C. Clarke's HAL 9000 in the film *2001: A Space Odyssey* (1968), and Douglas Adams created Marvin the Paranoid Android in *The Hitchhiker's Guide to the Galaxy* (2005), both realized as deep-toned, thoughtful, male voices.

And that's the point: these are all *voices*, rather than accents, specifically. What I mean is, I don't think I know of a robot that was clearly regional – a Texan robot, for example. We bestow our robots with human form, but keep their voices asexual. It's the same with lifts, or transport announcements. We don't want our inanimate objects to have too much of a personality, perhaps because otherwise we'll end up with more depressed machines like Marvin, or Adams' later creation, the lift that's afraid of heights.

Our cartoon characters certainly behave like humans – Donald Duck wraps a towel around his waist when he leaves the bath (despite never wearing trousers) – but tend to have an unplaceable, accessible accent. My favourite, the Road Runner, was voiced by Paul Julian (and chased by the mostly voiceless Wile E. Coyote), the latter, like all the Warner Bros creations, was the product of Mel Blanc's vocal manipulations. While I can hear Bugs Bunny's voice as clear as my mother's in my head, I couldn't tell you where Bugs grew up, or what his accent is. The wonderful Marvin the Martian's voice was peculiarly high-pitched, nasal, and sounded pitifully human when he cried out for his Illudium Q-36 Explosive Space Modulator. Alien or not, the makers want audiences to hear Us and not Them.

Aliens seem to come in two forms: friendly and hostile. Both types are usually easy to spot by their voices, although Tim Burton mixed it up in his beautifully simple, idiosyncratic way, by having his Martians in *Mars Attacks!* (1996) only ever say, '*Utt! Utt tut utt!*' in a strangled, almost metallic voice, so on first encounter it wasn't clear if they were friend or foe.

There rarely seems to be occasion where we find out what someone from the planet Betelgeuse might actually sound like.*

DAVID Friendly or hostile? Here's an experiment anyone can do. Set up a scenario in which humans are piloting a

---

* Portrayed so far by Geoffrey McGivern (from London), David Dixon (Derby), and Mos Def (Brooklyn), Douglas Adams' alien from a small planet somewhere in the vicinity of Betelgeuse, was called Ford Prefect, and was unusual, but definitely human.

spacecraft towards a planet in an alien galaxy. The only thing they know about the planet is that it's populated by two races. One race is known to be friendly; the other is known to be belligerent. Information about the names of the two races has just come through from Earth, but Mission Control doesn't know which name belongs to which race. The crew's task is to guess the correspondence. Here are the names:

the Lamonians   the Graks

I've never met anyone who couldn't do this. Everybody says the Lamonians must be the friendly race. You couldn't have a name like Grak and be pleasant, people say.

This way of thinking about sounds is called 'sound symbolism'. Some sounds in a language evidently have warm, friendly, comfortable, pleasant associations. Some sounds are the opposite. In English, resonant continuing consonants like *m*, *n*, and *l* are rated warmly, especially when they're used in a sequence, such as the three-syllable *Lamonians*. Short, sharp sounds such as *k*, *g*, and *t* are rated more harshly, especially when they're used in a single syllable, as in *Graks*.

There's no hard-and-fast rule, of course. These are tendencies, not rules. But film writers have to think about these issues when creating an alien language. Are the aliens going to be good guys? If so, the director will want the language to sound pleasant to human ears, which will mean using softer sounds, as in Na'vi, the language used by the inhabitants of Pandora in the 2009 movie *Avatar*. Are they bad guys? Then a harsher sounding language will be likely, full of sharp-sounding guttural consonants, as with Klingon in *Star Trek*.

How do you invent an alien accent? It isn't as easy as you might think. It's not enough just to take some sounds from a well-known modern language and twist them a bit. If the beings look really alien, and behave in an alien way, then they should sound alien too. On the other hand, one has to be practical. The accent mustn't be so different or difficult that it can't be easily pronounced by the characters.

Alien-language inventors usually base their creation on existing human languages, choosing the less common sounds and combining them in novel ways. The Ewok language in *Star Wars*, for example, was based on Tibetan; and if you listen carefully to scenes where aliens congregate you'll hear bits of Quechua, Finnish, and other languages in the babble of conversation. As for learning an alien accent: the author of a Klingon guide rightly says, following notions of best practice in foreign language teaching, 'The best way to learn to pronounce Klingon with no trace of a Terran or other accent is to become friends with a group of Klingons and spend a great deal of time socializing with them.'

Of course, film directors are also aware that aliens may not use anything remotely like the human system of speaking. Astrolinguists, as they're sometimes called, speculate about the possibilities of cosmic communication. If and when the search for extraterrestrial intelligence (SETI) receives evidence of intelligent life, alien speech may be quite unlike anything used by humans on earth. It might use the infrared scale. It might use musical tones, as in *Close Encounters of the*

Third Kind. The Wookies of *Star Wars* sound as if they're growling. Droids such as R2-D2 use a complex system of beeps and whistles. Gone are the days when every alien, from Martians to Daleks, gave the impression of being a native speaker of English.

But what happens when the plot does require a conversation between aliens and humans? What accents should the aliens have then? Friendly aliens usually have a standard English accent. They speak like us, therefore they like us. Enemy aliens follow the opposite principle: introduce features which are as far away as possible from normal English – though not so far that the speech will be unintelligible. It sounds like an impossible task, but in fact it's easily solved when we think of the two dimensions that comprise an accent.

One dimension has the segments of speech – the vowels and the consonants – which make up syllables, words, and sentences. The other dimension has the tones of voice – the effects of pitch, loudness, speed, and rhythm – that make utterances sound different. The two sides are succinctly summarized in the old maxim: 'It ain't what you say but the way that you say it.' And this suggests how they complement each other: the chief job of the vowels and consonants is to make speech intelligible; the chief job of tones of voice is to convey emotions.

So, faced with the task of devising a voice to make Daleks intelligible yet super-evil, the recipe is plain. Let them use normal vowels and consonants, so that they're understandable, but take away every feature of intonation and rhythm that reminds you of normal human English. Make them speak in a monotone with abnormal rising lilts. Add a staccato rhythm. Not 'ex*ter*minate' but 'ex-ter-min-ate', with each syllable prominent. Lengthen the vowels more than they would normally sound. Add a touch of haranguing loudness. And introduce a metallic voice quality that no human voice could possibly achieve.

Most enemy aliens using English have a deviant voice quality that affects the way they speak. They can sound hoarse, or nasal, or creaky, or breathy, or all of these together. Weird intonations and rhythms are commonplace. *Doctor Who*'s Cybermen, who have no emotions at all, compete with Daleks for monotone and staccato. Zygons speak in low-pitched, hissing, whispering voices. And altering an accent can have devastating effects. In 'The Robots of Death' (from the days when the Doctor was played by Tom Baker) the villain is destroyed by one of his own robots when the Doctor's assistant releases some helium gas, causing his voice to become high-pitched and squeaky. As a result he is no longer recognized by his robots, who turn on him and kill him. This may well be the only recorded case of an accent modification actually being fatal.

Cartoon characters face a similar problem to aliens. If they're human, all they need is a 'funny voice', which usually takes the form of a recognizable standard accent with some of its features exaggerated – the voice becomes deeper, or falsetto, or more nasal. Sometimes it takes only a single consonant or vowel switch to create the effect, as with Elmer Fudd's substitution of *w* for *r* – 'Kill the wabbit!' A surprising number of cartoon humans would benefit from a course in speech therapy.

As would cartoon animals. Porky Pig has a stutter that definitely needs treatment. Daffy Duck needs his slushy *s* consonants sorted. Bugs Bunny is hypernasal. Goofy could do with some help to get round his habit of swallowing sounds. And as for Donald Duck . . . He speaks using an air-flow that builds up within the cheeks. It's technically called a 'buccal' voice, and it's quite difficult for a human to do. A duck speech therapist would probably say it was normal.

Sometimes speech is dispensed with altogether, and we're left with only intonation patterns to convey attitudes, as with Mr Bean. An entire conversation can be carried on, if necessary, using only melodic patterns. Older readers will remember the BBC television animation of the early 1970s, *Clangers* – a family of mouse-like creatures, living inside a small planet, who spoke only in whistles. The narrator (the writer Oliver Postgate) interpreted the whistles for the viewer, but much of the meaning was already well conveyed by the intonation.

[B – A new series is commissioned for 2015. Can. Not. Wait.]

Robots are different. Because they've been made by humans, they reflect human characteristics, with most having faces, arms, legs – and voices. The accents their creators choose for them usually reflect the standard educated accents of the time. C-3PO in *Star Wars* has an elegant RP, voiced by Anthony Daniels (born in Wiltshire). The robot butler in *Robot and Frank,* voiced by Peter Sarsgaard (born in Illinois), has a gentle American accent. Computer voices are the same. HAL 9000 in *2001* talks a soft, calm North American (Canadian this time, from Douglas Rain).

Talking robots and computers haven't been around for very long, but their creators have already begun to realize that they need to think carefully about the accents they give them. Humans have strong views about accents, as we see throughout this book, and are ready to rate each other's qualities – rightly or wrongly – on the basis of the way they speak. It wouldn't be surprising, then, to find these ratings transferred to interactions with machines. How trustworthy is your robot? How intelligent? How sexy?

A survey carried out by the British hands-free car-kit firm Bury Technologies in 2009 showed that almost half of the almost 3,000 people they asked found regional accents to be sexy. Irish and Scots came top. One in six said they had dated someone purely because they liked their accent. Another one in six admitted they were irritated or embarrassed by their partner's accent, and 5 per cent of those questioned said they had dumped someone in the past because of it.

It's also a matter of credibility. Certain accents seem, in popular perception, to suit certain kinds of subject matter. Ask someone which accent they associate most with, say, agriculture, theology, or space exploration, and they will tell you. The associations seem more to do with their experience of these subjects on radio and television, than with anything encountered in real life. I recently heard my (British)-English-speaking eight-year-old grandson counting down as he prepared a toy rocket for lift-off. His accent was perfect Houston.

The pleasantness or otherwise of an accent can affect you in all kinds of ways. The makers of GPS audio car navigation systems soon learned that the choice of accent can affect the driver's concentration and state of mind. As one firm puts it, 'Awful GPS voices make for awful drives.' That's why firms give you options, and go in for celebrity voices such as David Hasselhoff (*Knight Rider*), Kim Cattrall (*Sex and the City*), and Homer Simpson. Personally, I would prefer Shakespearean OP.

So, your robot's accent will affect the way you relate to it, and researchers are beginning to explore the issues. A 2011 study from New Zealand gave three synthesized accents – British, American, and New Zealand – to a health-care robot whose job was to assist with blood-pressure measurement. New Zealand listeners rated the robot's overall performance as higher when it had the local accent compared to the other voices. You'll trust your robot more if it speaks like you. We need accommodating robots.

It's early days, but one thing is clear: voiced equipment is going to become increasingly routine, and the choice of accent(s) has to be seriously considered by manufacturers. It applies to everything – recorded voices at the other end of a telephone, intelligent personal assistants such as Apple's Siri, unintelligent advisers such as those who are limited to telling you which floor you've reached in a lift. The manufacturers want us to take them seriously; but that isn't always possible. I was in a lift in Manchester the other day, and the recorded voice had one of the poshest British accents imaginable. Everyone in the lift laughed when they heard it. I'm sure that wasn't the maker's intention.

Those who decide on robot voices need to be aware of the cultural trends in accent preferences, discussed earlier. If it benefits companies to employ people with certain accents in call centres, or use these accents in television commercials, it will benefit them to think about programming their robots in similar ways. Or at least giving listeners the choice. After all, an accent isn't just about the appeal of the sound, it can affect intelligibility.

In 2001 there was an interesting story about the new tram service between Wolverhampton and Birmingham. The tram-stop announcements were read out in a recorded RP, evoking widespread derision and complaints. In the case of the Bradley Lane stop in Bilston, to the east of Wolverhampton, the announcer got the pronunciation completely wrong, saying *Bradley* as if rhyming with *badly*, whereas the locals call the area *Braidley*. A Midland Metro spokesman said at the time, 'We were inundated with requests to change it.' And they did.

Machines aren't yet brilliant at speaking or understanding accents, but they're improving. Anyone with a strong regional accent who's tried to use a speech-recognition-enabled device knows the problem. These days there are many such devices. Since 2001, Amtrak, the US passenger rail system, has had a telephone-booking service, with a female voice who calls herself Julie offering schedules, reservations, and train status reports. There are washing machines, wheelchairs, toilets, and heating systems that can respond to the voice now. This isn't just for fun. They play an important role in assisting disabled and elderly people.

Progress has been amazing in the past ten years or so, but there's still some way to go. No system is yet perfect when speech commands are spoken too quickly, or where a lot of background noise interferes, or where there are many proper names. They all have serious limitations to do with the amount of vocabulary they can handle, or the complexity of the sentences put to them. We're not yet at the stage where we can have a friendly chat with our toilet. But it's not that far off.

As for accents: a few years ago, I was employed as a consultant by a speech-recognition firm with the instruction to try to 'break' their latest piece of equipment. What they meant was: speak our commands with every accent at your disposal, and see if the machine fails to recognize them. I tried, and the equipment got them right about 90 per cent of the time. This was an excellent result. On the other hand, not all systems are yet so efficient. A few years ago, my wife and I were driving late at night and called a hotel to make a booking. It was an automatic voice response, which wanted our name, address, and credit-card details to make the booking. No matter how we tried, we couldn't get it to accept that there was such a name as Crystal. We gave up, and found a hotel that was staffed by a human being.

ACCENTS LIVING

BEN   As I write, there's an annoying TV advert with a guy using a Brummie accent, and a reassuringly friendly, let's-band-together advert for a bank with a perky female Edinburgh accent.

Laying my accent cards on the table, my favourites in Britain are (in no particular order) Yorkshire, Edinburgh, Somerset, Dublin, and North Wales, and the ones I'm less disposed towards are Cockney, Birmingham, Belfast, and South Wales (I did grow up in the north of the province, after all). Before the hate mail comes, I say *less disposed* – I love them all, and my disposition has nothing to do with the people who speak with those accents. I'm considering a sound quality that resonates with me for some reason, like a preference for jazz over blues.

I'm not going to give better grace to John Lee Hooker or Ray Charles, Nina Simone or Aretha Franklin, Dickens or Austen, Shakespeare or Chaucer. One isn't better than the other, all are terrific at what they do, and one person's meat is rarely a total crowd pleaser. Shakespeare would have sounded like Dickens to Chaucer. No wait, Chaucer would have sounded like Dickens to Shakespeare.

Although I suppose Dad would say that's not true either: Shakespeare would have had terrible trouble understanding Chaucer's accent, even though he and all his actors, and his audiences, would have known Father Chaucer's tales well, a sort of equivalent of our faerie tales and nursery once-upon-a-times.

The arrival of the separate and distinct stronger brogues in London was noticed and written about by the literary greats Dickens, Hardy, and Brontë, until the twentieth century, when audio and visual communication networks open up, accents begin to meld and flatten out and everybody becomes a critic.

On the Internet Movie Database, there's a piece of trivia for the 1998 film *There's Something About Mary*:

> Lee Evans' British accent in the movie was characterized by a film critic as quite possibly the worst fake British accent in a movie he had ever heard. Lee Evans is in fact British, however his normal accent is the Bristol accent of British as opposed to the snobbish posh version he used in the movie. While this means his accent is in all actuality not fake, it was exaggerated for the role.

Ouch. Wait. What? I hadn't noticed that, and would argue Cheadle's Cockney accent in *Ocean's Eleven* (2001) trumps Evans. I think I've a good ear now – I can hear when an accent from a place I'm familiar with goes awry, but I'm no accent detective. James Bond, in *GoldenEye* (1995), the reboot of the film franchise, however, seems to be just that:

JB – The name's Bond. James Bond.

XZO – Xenia Zaragevna Onatopp.

JB – Onatopp?

XZO – Onatopp.

JB – Your accent . . . Georgian?

XZO – Very good, Mr Bond. You've been to Russia.

JB – (shrugs) Not recently.

Talking to someone with a Russian accent, perceiving that they're from a particular part of the biggest country in the world when you're not from there, is a pretty neat skill. (Personally, and I'm not proud about this, I have to Google-Maps Georgia.)

I *can* hear whether someone's Liverpool or Manchester, Glasgow or Edinburgh, Belfast or Dublin, Yorkshire or Lancashire, though I struggle sometimes to discern America from Canada. I'd really struggle even to name two regions in Soviet Russia, let alone hear the difference between Tbilisi and Volgograd. Surely for that you'd need to have lived there, or heard both accents a lot.

That said, as we've seen, you can live somewhere for years, and your neighbours will only ever hear you as a newcomer, but go home and your friends say, *Oh you've got such an accent . . .*

But we've somehow inherited the idea that all accents of a foreign language are the same, that there's broad 'Russian', 'French', 'German', and 'General American' (an accent currently widely taught and that sits, geographically, nowhere). When I learned Spanish I had one accent from the language tapes I'd bought and then developed – I suppose you could call it – a 'detailed' accent from spending time down in Granada, *thhh* instead of a *s*, as in *And-a-loo-thhh-ee-ah* instead of *And-a-loo-see-ah*.*

I used to helplessly drown in the Welsh sound, and now I can quickly tell what part of Wales someone is from. My gaining a Welsh accent when I was a seven-year-old immigrant to Holyhead from Wokingham became about surviving the playground, and then about being accepted when I returned home from university (doffing the Lancashire flecks I'd since picked up); and then hearing or speaking a Welsh accent became about being homesick in London.

My adopted-native Welsh accent makes me feel warmer, safe, more heartfelt, even. It makes me feel like I should go out and discuss the best road route to Llanfairfechan with someone. I'd hate to lose it, even if I don't use it all the time.

A quick cycle through daily, then weekly, then life-through-a-year, and I realize I only ever switch from my modified RP to a North Walian sound in a finite number of instances, rising from a fairly strong sound (1) to as thick as syrup (5):

1. when I'm home in Wales

2. when I randomly bump into another Welsh person

3. when I'm abroad and I know the locals aren't big fans of English tourists

---

*   A common phonetic quality that many Spaniards naturally use.

4. when I'm recording a voice-over and am asked to 'do a Welsh accent'

5. and when I'm abroad and I randomly bump into another Welsh person. Then it goes off the scale almost into caricature, such is the mutual joy of hearing someone from Home.

The North Welsh accent to me is a mixture of Welsh, with flecks of Dublin, and flecks of Scouse. But Scouse itself, for me, has flecks of Irish, Mancunian, and . . . something else that has more to do with the character of the city-dweller.

Andrew Jack, accent coach to film actors, interviewed on the BBC Radio 4's *Film Programme* in February 2014, did a whistle-stop tour of accents of the UK in a minute and twenty-three seconds, non-stop, slipping effortlessly from one to the next. I can't reproduce the accents here, but his descriptions hint at the variety.

RP is the great communicator . . . but as soon as you deviate from the base and go into London speech, for example, then you lose a bit of the communication, as Cockney is based in East Anglia . . . Suffolk, Norfolk, Cambridgeshire . . . and this is often by actors confused with the West Country when the *arrs* come in and you get Dorset and Somerset . . . then you get into Cornwall . . . Devon's slightly different, it goes into the nose a bit more . . . then you go up to Yorkshire, it's nice if you get a word that's got one of the predominant sounds in it like *Yorrrkshire* . . . then you cross the Pennines into Lancashire when it gets more flexible and fluid in the mouth . . . Liverpool is there too, y'know, it's Scouse, it's a mixture of all kinds of sounds . . . one of those is North-ern Irish, with the rising inflections . . . but you don't get the rising inflections down in Dublin where it has that poetic quality . . . which is sometimes thought of as not-that-different from Highlands speech, which is also quite poetic and almost Scandinavian . . . and then you come down to Glasgow, and the lowlands of Scotland where you get glottal stops and things like that . . . and you come down the west coast and you're in Wales . . . North Wales where it's breathy . . . and down into South Wales where you get much heavier, and Welsh people who sometimes even sound a bit drunk . . .

Those of you from Britain will probably be able to hear the varying sounds as you read through a passage like this. And it gives the lie to those from around the world who think that only one accent belongs to Britain.

But could a single national accent ever happen? Or could the world's varieties of English simmer down to just four or five general accents? Will Milwaukee, Manchester, and Canberra drown out their neighbours?

Will the accent we use be, in effect, our identity papers? Will the norm be to have an accent for your home, one for your work, one for your friends, and one for global com-munication? Or will our homes be fully virtually connected, our work international, and our friends global? Or has that already happened?

What happens if all the littler accents die out?

Pops?

ACCENTS DYING

DAVID All accents change their character over time. That's what history teaches us. And not just history: living memory too. We need only listen to our grandchildren or grandparents, or even to our children and parents, as we saw in our Introduction. And every now and then we hear archive programmes on the radio or television which remind us how differently people spoke once upon a time. As the villain in *Aladdin* might have said: new accents for old.

Some accents have indeed disappeared. The underlying theme of this book is the way accents reflect identity. So, clearly, when an old way of life dies out, the accent associated with that time will die out along with it. It doesn't happen immediately, because accents are extremely resilient. Parents pass their accents on to their children, so we hear echoes of the older way of speaking long after the parents have passed away. But a generation later, the changes introduced by the young people will have noticeably altered it; and within two or three generations, we would probably say that the old accent has gone.

The new generation is speaking with its own accent. The

interesting question is whether this accent retains local distinctiveness, just as its predecessors did, or whether there has been what phoneticians call a 'levelling'. Levelling happens when one accent becomes influenced by another, so that it begins to sound like the other. If several accents do this, from different parts of the country, then it would feel as if everyone was beginning to talk in the same way. The total number of distinguishable accents in a country would then be less than it was before. That's what people mean when they talk about accents dying out. They think the diversity ain't what it used to be.

Estuary English

There's certainly some levelling taking place in Britain right now. Everybody notices it. In fact they've been noticing it for the past twenty years or so. The term 'Estuary English' arrived in the 1980s, and was seized upon by the media as a convenient label to describe one of the levelling trends that was taking place. The estuary in question was the River Thames, and the accent was one which people could hear developing not just in London but in all the nearby counties, such as Essex, Hertfordshire, and Kent. It seemed to be a mixture of RP and Cockney. It came about because two major changes in lifestyle were happening at once.

There was, firstly, an upmarket change. Many whose families had long lived in London, and who spoke with a Cockney accent, found they could afford to move from their East End homes to the suburbs, where they felt they would have a better quality of life. Many had no choice but to do so, following the London devastation of World War II. Some went further afield, into the Home Counties. They brought their Cockney accent with them, but once settled, they began to accommodate to the local accents they encountered in their new community. This being the south-east, RP was everywhere. Gradually, their London accent picked up some of the features of RP.

At the same time as this was happening, there was a change in the other direction. Increasing numbers of people from outside London, and who spoke with the local accent of their community, began to commute to jobs in the south-east, and especially in the capital. Some found they could afford to live in the city, or even to have a second home there. Some began a daily commute. With the development of the motorway system and faster rail travel, commuting distances increased. Birmingham to London in a couple of hours. Manchester to London not much more. Leeds to London likewise. They brought their local accents with them, but once settled in their new jobs, they began to accommodate to the new accents they encountered among their colleagues. This being London, Cockney-influenced accents were everywhere, as well as RP. Gradually, their accent picked up some of the features of what was happening in London. And at the end of their working day or week, they brought those features home with them.

Estuary English blended features of two accents, therefore – but it did so in various ways. There was never a single

Estuary English. Nor, of course, has there ever been a single RP. RP has always shown variations. Some speakers are very conservative, reflecting an older style of speech. Some are very modern, reflecting the latest speaking fashions. There's still a lot of variation. Listen to the way RP speakers say words like *cool* and *good*. Older speakers will have a strongly rounded vowel. Younger ones will tend to lose the rounding, so that they sound more like 'cull' and 'gud'.

Estuary English shows this kind of variation too. Some speakers use more Cockney features than RP; some have more RP than Cockney. And of course some introduce features from a local accent that is neither RP nor Cockney, so we get a three-way mix. But there are certain features that most Estuary speakers share, such as the replacement of *th* by *f* or *v*, in such words as *youth*, *thanks*, and *bother*. Lauren, the schoolgirl television character created by Catherine Tate, had a catch-phrase which was universally reported as 'Am I bovvered?' *Bovvered* was voted Word of the Year in 2006. And we hear *f* for *th* in parts of the country these days where it never used to be, as the example of Glasgow and *EastEnders* illustrated.

Another widespread Estuary feature is the increasing use of glottal stops in place of *t*. A glottal stop happens when the vocal cords come together and are suddenly released, as they do for a cough. It's been a noticeable feature of Cockney for generations, with words like *bottle* and *hot* coming out as *bo'le* and *ho'*. We saw earlier that replacing the middle *t* by a glottal stop remains an important feature of Cockney. Estuary speakers on the whole don't (yet) say *bo'le*. But they do replace the *t* at the end of a word, and say such things as *ge'*, *le'*, and *ho'*.

Actually, this isn't a completely novel effect. RP speakers have been 'dropping their *t*s' for a long time. The phonetician Daniel Jones remarks on it in the 1920s, and we can hear it in early speech recordings, even in people who speak in a voice we would describe as 'refined'. But most RP speakers have learned to articulate their *t*s at the ends of words. And the models of accent fashion certainly did so. Queen Elizabeth, for example, in her speech to the Australian parliament in 1954, clearly articulates the consonant in such phrases as *great realm*.

So it is a significant change to hear modern RP speakers regularly dropping their *t*s in informal speech at the end of such words as *hot*, *get*, and *great*, or in the middle of such words as *football* and *Gatwick*. Princes William and Harry do, for example, partly reflecting their time in contact with other accents in their professional roles. They can code-switch, though – switching into a more traditional RP when occasion demands, such as reading a speech. When Prince William was about to leave Anglesey, at the end of his stay at RAF Valley, his address at the Anglesey County Show begins with some informal remarks, where final *t*s are dropped; but not a single *t* is dropped when reading his prepared text.

So there is some widespread levelling in the UK at the moment, but this doesn't amount to a total replacement of one accent by another. Rather, what we hear is one accent being coloured by another. Young people in Glasgow still sound Glaswegian even if they do replace *th* by *f*. The new features are changing the character of the accent, certainly, but the local identity is still being distinctively expressed, especially in the intonation. And RP has been affected in the same way. When people hear radio or television announcers speaking in a regional accent, they are quick to identify it as Scottish or Welsh or whatever; but what they fail to notice is that the accents have been pulled in the direction of RP. It is accent colouring rather than accent replacement. Phoneticians call it 'modified RP'. It would be an impossible broadcasting situation otherwise: a really broad regional accent would interfere with comprehension for anyone not used to it. That was why Lord Reith (a Scot) went for RP at the BBC in the first place. It was the accent most likely to be understood by the majority of listeners. Modified forms of RP are just as comprehensible.

Accents in music

A good example of where we hear a lot of accent levelling is in music. It's fairly unusual for a singer to have a clearly identifiable accent. There are several reasons for this. The first is phonetic. A number of the main identifying features of a regional accent tend to disappear when singing – the intonation (obviously, as a melody replaces it), the speech rhythm, and vowel length (for many syllables are elongated). Vowel quality is also often affected, especially in classical singing, where vowels are articulated with greater openness than in everyday speech. Listen to opera singers singing in English.

Can you tell which part of a country they're from? Probably not. You might just be able to tell their nationality – Italian or German, say, or even British vs American, but even that is usually impossible.

All of this can affect the artistry. Here's a comment from singer Billy Bragg, saying that a London accent (which he uses while singing) forces a singer to approach melody differently:

> You can't sing something like 'Tracks Of My Tears' in a London accent. The cadences are all wrong. It's also difficult to sing harmonies in a London accent. And you can't sustain syllables for long.

It's not possible to generalize from this, because accents have very different norms – different rhythms and rates of articulation, for example – but it's interesting to hear a singer reflecting on the issues. Some singing groups have too, where the question of accent raises an issue of voice blending. The King's Singers, for example (who generally sing in RP), answer a Frequently Asked Question on their website:

> We are often asked whether we have auditioned non-British candidates. We have! However, every successful candidate (so far!) has been British. This has a lot to do with our concerns over blending, and the way vowels are shaped. The way Americans or Germans speak, for example, makes blending with 5 other Brits very difficult.

A further reason for accent levelling in singing is social. Some singers want to drop their regional accent, because they want to sing like the fashionable mainstream. This has been especially noticeable in popular music since the early days of rock 'n' roll. Singers everywhere imitated Bill Haley and Elvis, and many still do. A mid-Atlantic hybrid quickly emerged, which levelled natural regional features. From his singing, who would ever guess where Cliff Richard comes from? Or Sting, Rod Stewart, Tom Jones, or Elton John? They are all likely to lengthen the vowel in *love* so that it comes out as 'lurve', regardless of how they say it in their everyday speech. They are likely to pronounce the *r* in such words as *girl*, even though they may not normally do this. *Top* is likely to come out more like 'tap', *my* more like 'mah', and *better* more like 'bedder'.

However, it's perfectly possible for singers to retain an individual accent, if they want to, and many do. In fact, they've been doing it for years. If we listen to recordings of music-hall days, we'll hear broad Cockney, Lancashire, Scots, Irish, and others. You could hardly get more Cockney, for example, than in such songs as 'Any Old Iron' or 'Boiled Beef and Carrots'.

And now there are signs of modern pop music returning to its accent roots. The Mersey sound was an early development. A Liverpudlian accent regularly stands out in the Beatles – such as (in 'Penny Lane') *customer* with a rounded first vowel and words like *there* and *wear* (in 'Only a Northern Song') with a central vowel (rhyming with *her*). I recall Paul McCartney saying that the Beatles did experiment with singing in an American accent early on, but decided against it because it sounded ridiculous. Other early departures in the UK from an American-sounding norm (or, at least, a mid-Atlantic-sounding norm) were Tommy Steele and Joe Brown.

You can actually study the way in which an individual singer or group changes its accent over the years. A fascinating report by Peter Trudgill in 1980 examined the way in which the Beatles sounded out the *r* after a vowel – something that most American singers would always do. In 1963–4, in such songs as 'Please Please Me', almost 50 per cent of the words containing this feature had the *r* sounded. By the time of the *Sergeant Pepper* album in 1967, this had fallen to less than 5 per cent. Note that the use of the feature was never totally consistent. That's normal. When singers copy Americans, they get the accent sometimes right, sometimes wrong. But over the years the Beatles' singing voices show that they are leaving the mid-Atlantic way behind and starting to sound more consistently British.

It's been a widespread trend, heard again in the London accents of Ian Dury, Chas & Dave, and Lily Allen, and the rather more gentrified tones of Anthony Newley. The Streets' Mike Skinner's accent is so noticeable (with its glottal stops, replacement of *th* by *f*, and other Cockney features) that it has been called Mockney. The accents of the Celtic areas of the British Isles are often heard. Listen for example to 'Daddy's Gone' from Glasvegas and you'll hear several local Scottish features, such as a fronted *ou* in *you* (like the vowel in French *tu*), an *e* vowel in the first syllable of *sitting*, and plenty of glottal stops.

Glottal stops are one of the things to listen out for, actually: you'll hear them in groups from different parts of the UK, such as Futurehead and The Rakes. Listen out too for the *r* after a vowel in Irish accents, as heard in, say, Mary Coughlan (from the South) and Snow Patrol (from the North). And of course in rapping we regularly get a distinctive accent, because of the syllable-timed rhythm. But my impression is that, rapping aside, in hardly any case do singers use a consistent regional accent throughout the whole song. Mixed accents seem to be the norm.

I hear a very different spectrum when I listen to folk singers. By 'folk singers' I mean traditional singers who are amateurs (or who developed their style as amateurs), and those 'revival' singers who copy traditional singers. Several revert to a less modified variant of their local accent when singing songs with (for them) local associations. The label 'folk' also includes singer-songwriters who compose texts to resemble local speech and perform them with local accents – as in the many country music singers who reflect accents of Tennessee. A performer with a huge popular following who started off in this 'folk' idiom is Billy Connolly, whose accent has never (I think) been described as 'mixed'. A less stellar but still very popular performer was Jake Thackeray. His singing accent followed his spoken accent in both the regional features he chose to preserve and the features he chose to modify. And Roger Davies sings about Huddersfield in Yorkshire in a totally Huddersfieldian way. So levelling isn't the whole story.

Global accents

While all this has been going on, something else has been happening which answers the question 'Are accents disappearing?' in a very different way: the emergence of new accents following the establishment of English as a global language. English is now spoken by over two thousand million people around the world. That total includes the well-known and widespread accents of the British Isles and North America, and of other parts of the world where English-speaking populations have been long established, such as Australia, New Zealand, South Africa, and the subcontinent of India. But alongside these, we have heard in the past century a range of accents that identify countries where English has come to be spoken as an official language or is being taught as the main foreign language, such as Japan, China, Nigeria, Ghana, Zimbabwe, Kenya, Singapore . . . and indeed it would be possible to give a list of over fifty countries where English is now so much a part of the society that the accents heard there are as valid an index of the speaker's identity as any heard in Britain or the USA.

When we think globally, the answer to the 'disappearance' question is definitely 'No'. On the contrary, the number of English accents in the world is growing. And this conclusion is reinforced when we listen to what is happening not only *in* those countries but in places such as the UK and the USA, where people *from* those countries have increasingly arrived as immigrants during the twentieth century. They bring their accents with them, and over time these modify as they come into contact with the accents of the places where they eventually live. Go to Liverpool these days, and you will not just hear a Scouse accent; you will hear Chinese Scouse, Indian Scouse, Bangladeshi Scouse, and so on. The same is true all over the English-speaking world, with the biggest cities exhibiting the greatest diversity. The hundreds of languages spoken in places such as London, Birmingham, Boston, and New York mean that a walk down any main street will bring to the ear an extraordinary diversity of English accents.

We'd expect these new ethnic accents to be coloured by the accents of the host country, when the immigrants settle down. Surprisingly, however, some of the traditional British accents have gone in the other direction, with the speakers picking up features of the immigrants' speech patterns. One of the earliest signs of this was the way young British people, impressed by the syllable-by-syllable ('rat-a-tat') rhythms of rapping and hip-hop, were quick to imitate them and then to incorporate some of the rhythmicality into their everyday speech. And there have now been several studies showing that the speech of young East London Cockney speakers has been influenced by immigrants, especially from Bangladesh.

There is no sign of a slowdown in the spread of English as a global language. And we seem to be moving away from a climate in which only certain English accents (chiefly RP and General American) were viewed as being acceptable targets for foreign learners. Today an international conference or business meeting will have participants who produce totally intelligible English while speaking in an accent that just as clearly shows their country of origin. Some English learners worry about this. 'I'd love to lose my foreign accent and sound just like a native speaker,' they say. To which I answer, 'Why? Why do you want to lose your identity?' And I advise them to be proud of their accent, in just the same way as I would tell people in Britain's regions to be proud of the way they speak, and not feel so insecure that they look for alternatives. As long as learners can communicate clearly and effectively, native speakers need ask for no more.

BEN'S EP-EE-LOG

When I was seventeen, my father gave me my first driving lessons, and one morning while out terrorizing the roads of rural North Wales, he asked, 'Could you make a U-turn?'

I replied, 'Can I make a ewe turn? No, but I can make its eyes water.'

I just about managed to pull over. An accent joke nearly killed us with laughter.

I'm going to hand over to my father here, because while accents are something I use, both for work and for play, I naturally see them more fleetingly than he. I certainly notice them more often than when I notice I'm breathing, as my conscious mind takes over from my autonomic system, but I pay them less attention than, well, a man who's been fascinated by them all his life, really.

That's why I wanted to write this book with my father. Other than the joy of getting to turn one's parent into a colleague, and indeed a friend, the opportunity of exploring one of my father's passions was irresistible.

Memories of Dad telling me Edinburgh was voted the most popular accent by customers calling call centres, or nearly getting beaten up by a drunken Irishman who thought that Dad was taking the mick, rather than subconsciously practising the linguistic art of accommodation.

Then, knocking on seventy—

[D – mid-sixties!]

Liar – and developing Shakespeare's Original Pronunciation, a new-old field of study that truly breaks new ground in an area where finding a metaphorical gap on the shelf is now so very hard, because so much has already been said about the most overwritten, over-analysed man of words . . . his work is something I can only admire with a soft headshake, and honestly gives me a moment to pause, and take a deep breath.

Every single time he tells me something is impossible, I know he only says it to spur me on.

He taught me to parallel park, to think laterally, and that nothing is ever really 'impossible'. Not even an accent map.

DAVID'S EP-I-LOG

It's been an extraordinary couple of decades, really. Developments have taken place remarkably quickly, and a book like this one I hope will help people get a more informed sense of what has been going on, and to understand better what's involved when talking about accents.

It's easy to see now, looking back, why there have been so many changes. Not only have accents themselves changed, but attitudes towards them have also changed. We're talking sociology now, not phonetics, of course. If accents reflect identity, then popular attitudes to them will change as perceptions of those identities change. And what social changes there have been! We need only think of the new sense of equality, and respect for diversity, that arose from the breakdown of old attitudes to race and gender; or the replacement of the old heritage-based class system by one in which people achieve prestige through merit and economic status. The amount of social diversity itself increased, following the post-war growth in immigration. And all these trends have altered our attitude towards the 'accents of others'.

Sociolinguists do attitude studies as follows. They play

people a recording of a text spoken in a number of different accents – ideally by the same person, so that the same voice quality is maintained throughout (some actors are very good at this). Then they ask listeners to answer a questionnaire about the person imagined to be behind the accent. The questions can be anything. Is the speaker honest? Is he (or she) intelligent? Would you buy a used car from this speaker? Would you like your child to marry this speaker?

The results are always illuminating, and never more so than over the past twenty or thirty years. Carry out an experiment like that in the 1980s, and the results would be clear: RP got all the positive values. RP speakers could only be educated, honest, respectable, intelligent, and definitely marriageable. Regional accents would get a lot of negative values. Would you buy a used car from someone with a Cockney accent? Probably not. Would a Birmingham speaker be likely to have committed a crime? We talked about that particular hot potato earlier.

Today, the polarities have significantly reversed. Regional voices tend to get far more positive responses than RP – which in turn attracts more negative associations, such as 'distant' and 'customer-unfriendly'. Ben's voice agent confirmed that. But old prejudices and stereotypes die hard. There are still far too many reports of accent antagonism around, of accent misinterpretation, of people being made to feel inferior because of the way they talk – even to the extent of them seeking professional help from elocutionists to change their accent. But Henry Higgins wouldn't survive as an elocutionist today, because even in that profession times have changed.

In 2012 a British private tuition company, The Tutor Pages, issued a report headed, 'Elocution in the New Britain', in which they said they were receiving more requests for elocution lessons than for any other subject, and that demand had doubled. Inevitably, this was translated into media head-lines about 'soaring demand' and 'death of accents'. But it did show that there is still a great deal of prejudice towards some regional accents, especially in the West Midlands and Birmingham. The report concluded:

> Today's elocution teachers are responding to these trends not by seeking to take their students back to the days of The King's Speech. Most people who come to them for help no longer wish to acquire a cut-glass accent or learn to speak like the Queen. On the whole they wish to retain their accents but to develop a clearer, softer, or more authoritative voice.

That's the point. There are all sorts of reasons why people feel they need voice help. In some cases it's speed of speech that is the problem: they need to slow down. In others it's a desire for a different voice quality – a softer voice, for example, or one that is less breathy or creaky. (Some quite famous politicians have gone down that road – Margaret Thatcher's lowering of her pitch-range is a well-known instance.) In some cases it's anxiety over speaking in public, which is far more than a purely linguistic matter. In others it's a need to sound more confident, which again is not solely a linguistic matter. In yet others, it's the need for better breath control.

These problems affect all accents – RP included. It's perfectly possible for any speaker to lack confidence, speak too fast, or be phonetically unclear. Even professionals can be affected. There's the infamous 'dropped intonation' at the end of a radio presenter's sentence, where the voice falls and quietens so that one struggles to hear what is being said:

'That was the piano concerto in D major by . . .'

'The programme will be repeated next Thursday at . . .'

Or listen to some of the RP voices on public-address systems in airports, ferry terminals, and railway stations. I spent some weeks once giving voice lessons to the people who made the announcements on Stena ferries. Almost without exception, they spoke too quickly – regardless of the accent they had. The task was to slow them down, to get them to speak clearly, but not to change their accents, which were all otherwise perfectly intelligible. It's a widespread problem. On a ferry crossing recently, my wife and I looked at each other in blank incomprehension at some of the announcements. It's because the crew have said them so often that they unconsciously speed up, leaving their listeners way behind. Companies need to pay serious attention to the issue, if only for health and safety reasons.

Ben and I have written this book together because, in our different worlds, we have encountered issues to do with accents that range from the mildly worrying to the truly upsetting. It's time to leave that period in our linguistic history behind. We value accent diversity and we hate accent intolerance. We think those who are in positions of power especially need to be aware of the harm they can do if they fail to respect accents. We value an informed understanding of what accents are and the role they play in relation to individual identity and the formation of community, and we hate the ignorance about accents that leads to false stereotypes and harmful prejudices about individuals and communities. In short: we think people should be proud of their accent, whatever it is.

AND ABOUT OUR TITLE . . .

BEN   So, er, Dad – It kinda says on the back of the book: Did anyone ever say 'potahto'? You might want to actually *answer* that, you know, in case we get complaints, or emails, or people throwing things at us in the street . . .

DAVID   In fact, what George and Ira Gershwin originally wrote was 'You *like* potatoes', but the 'say' version has become the one everybody remembers because that's the verb used when the song starts:

> You say eether and I say iyther . . .

It's sung by Fred Astaire (Peter) and Ginger Rogers (Linda) in the 1937 film *Shall We Dance*. And did they dance! They come in with a quickstep, sit down to sing the song, and finish off with a virtuoso comic tap-dance duet before collapsing onto the grass. All on roller-skates! After that, imitating accents seems a piece of cake.

The pair have been deciding what to do about their proposed marriage. 'I don't know what to do,' says Linda. 'I don't either,' says Peter, pronouncing the word with the first syllable rhyming with *my* – *iyther*. Linda reacts scathingly. 'The word is either,' pronouncing it firmly as *eether*. Peter tries to soothe, but not very successfully:

> Peter: Alright, the word is eether. No use squabbling.
>   That won't get niyther of us any place.
> Linda (even more scathingly): The word is neether.

Cue song from Peter:

> You say eether and I say iyther,
> You say neether and I say niyther,
> Eether, iyther, neether, niyther,
> Let's call the whole thing off . . .
> You like potaytoes, and I like potahtoes,
> You like tomaytoes, and I like tomahtoes,
> Potaytoes, potahtoes, tomaytoes, tomahtoes,
> Let's call the whole thing off . . .

It's the short or 'flat' *a* vs the long or 'broad' *ah* that dominates the song. In later verses the two swap *pajamas* and *pajahmas*, *after* and *ahfter*, *lafter* and *lahfter*, *Havana* and *Havahna*, and *banana* and *banahna* – as well as the less familiar *oysters* and *ersters*.

What's going on? To modern ears, it sounds like a contrast between American and British English – but both the characters are American, so that can't be the reason. And while *tomayto* and *tomahto* are both well-known pronunciations, where on earth does *potahto* come from? Everybody says *potayto* now, on both sides of the Atlantic.

But a century ago it was very different. That long, far-back *ah* vowel had come into English around the end of the eighteenth century in Britain, and was beginning to be an important distinguishing feature of social class, with educated southerners living in long-vowelled *Bahth* and northerners, educated or not, having a short-vowelled *bath*. The long *ah* had been in regional speech for a long time before that, of course, and had travelled across from Britain on the *Mayflower* along with its short *a* counterpart, settling in several parts of America, such as Boston and the South. Even *potato* sometimes had the long *ah* in those days, echoing the original Spanish *patata*. And as the American population grew, and class distinctions became increasingly prominent and sensitive (not least between white and black speech), so the accent scenario became more varied.

By the end of the nineteenth century, usage was very mixed in the United States. A linguist observer of the 1870s, William D. Whitney, noted how the short *a* was beginning to replace the long *ah* in many words, such as *after* and *laugh*. By the 1930s, the long *ah* was being described as a speech affectation, used especially by upper-class women. The news-papers in the 1940s often refer to it. A *Boston Herald* editorial in 1944 was headed, 'An A for an R'.

H. L. Mencken, author of *The American Language*, writing in the 1940s, notes that *tomahto* was still being used in Boston and Virginia, 'and seems to be making some progress among the elegant elsewhere'. But he then tells a story about a Massachusetts representative who used *tomahto* during a meeting of a House committee, and was challenged by a fellow-representative who asked him if he meant *tomayto*. 'No,' replied the Massachusetts man, 'I mean *tomahto*.' His colleague then appealed to the Democratic majority on the committee, who decided in favour of *tomayto*.

Accent arguments can surface anywhere, as everyone has an accent and everyone has feelings about their own and other people's. Accents raise issues of personal and social identity – of who you are, where you come from, and where you belong. Whatever class distinctions a country has, accents reflect them. And accents can be used as a sign that people are getting to like each other or, as Peter and Linda felt, a good reason not to continue a relationship.

Actually, Peter and Linda are closer than they think. When Peter sings his verses, he says he likes *ah*. When Linda sings, she says she likes *ah* too. If they are going to not go ahead with their plan to marry, they need better reasons than blaming their accents.

[B – True. Just talking about the wedding schedule would be tricky.]

INDEX

In this book we tell the story of English accents through their regional locations, but if you'd like to find out where we encountered them, or the entertainers and other personalities who've used them, these indexes will guide you.

INDEX

INDEX

Radio, television, theatre, & film productions

INDEX